OLEG
IGNATYEV

SECRET WEAPON IN AFRICA

PROGRESS PUBLISHERS
MOSCOW

Translated from the Russian by *David Fidlon*
Designed by *Vladimir Fatekhov*

ОЛЕГ ИГНАТЬЕВ

Секретное оружие в Африке

На английском языке

First printing 1977

© Издательство «Прогресс» 1977

© Translation into English. Progress Publishers 1977

Printed in the Union of Soviet Socialist Republics

И $\frac{11104-046}{016(01)-77}$ 99—77

CONTENTS

The Last Sixteen Years

In the morning of November 10, 1975, Igor Uvarov, a TASS correspondent, Ryszard Kapuściński of the Polish Press Agency and I went from Hotel Tivoli in Luanda to the former gubernatorial palace to pick up invitations for the ceremony of the proclamation of Angola's independence.

Presenting us with the programme of festivities Comrade Costa of the Information Ministry suggested that we should not miss the "Veterans of 1961" torchlight procession which would take in the sites of the historic events of February 4 in Luanda, when almost fifteen years ago the people of Angola rose in arms against Salazar's colonialists and led by the MPLA began the fight for freedom and independence.

...Those who on that day in February 1961 launched the assault on the bastions of Portuguese colonialism in Angola now moved towards May First Square, their torches forming a blazing corridor in the darkness of the night. Thousands of people lined the streets cheering the heroes who had ignited a spark of hope in the hearts of the Angolan people in those grim days. The veterans marched through the streets of Luanda, but in other parts of the country the younger generation was locked in a life and death struggle with Angola's enemies who wanted to deprive the people of their newly-won independence.

The battle for freedom continued: the battle against the South African interventionists; the battle against the mercenaries of the fascist "Portuguese Liberation Army" and against Spanish, Belgian and American mercenaries who had taken part in massacring civilians, women and children in the Congo, Nigeria and Vietnam; the battle against the splitter puppet organisations FNLA and UNITA.

* * *

In the last months of 1975 and the first months of 1976, events in Angola made headline news. Angola was the leading theme at numerous international conferences, symposiums and discussions. In the capitalist countries bourgeois politicians of all ranks tried to convince public opinion of their impartiality towards Angola and her people, and prove that always and everywhere did they uphold her independence and had no special interests in Angola.

This chapter, which precedes the main narrative, is designed to give the reader an insight into the 1975 events in Angola, for it is impossible to understand the present without looking into the past. Angola's independence did not come into being all of a sudden, of its own accord. It was won in the course of a bitter and relentless struggle which lasted for many years, and as any other struggle it involved two sides, each striving for victory. On one side of the barricades were those who fought for an independent Angola and those who helped them in this struggle. On the other were their adversaries and those who helped them. There is only one way of getting an objective idea of the events in 1975 and 1976 and this is to recapitulate the past.

* * *

In December 1956 a manifesto was circulated in many countries announcing the formation of an Angolan organisation Movimento Popular da Liberação da Angola (MPLA).

The Manifesto said in part: "Colonialism inoculated the microbes of destruction, hatred, decline, poverty, ignorance and reaction into the body of Angola. . . . This means that we have to mobilise the Angolan people and to fight on all fronts, under all circumstances in order to weaken imperialism and Portuguese colonialism, turn Angola into an independent country and form a democratic and popular Angolan government. This coalition government will unite all the forces which will fight to the finish, against Portuguese colonialism. At the head of this government of all anti-imperialist forces will stand the class of the working people.

"But Portuguese colonialism will not fall without a fight. Therefore the people of Angola can liberate themselves only by taking the path of revolutionary struggle. It will become the victorious path of creating a united front of all anti-imperialist forces in Angola irrespective of racial distinctions, social origin, religious belief and the individual make-up. It will be victorious thanks to the formation of a vast movement for the liberation of Angola."

When the Manifesto was published not many people promptly recognised the MPLA's leading role in the struggle against Portuguese colonial domination.

Although prominent Angolan intellectuals were members of the MPLA (it was the first organisation with a clear and comprehensive political programme), and it was universally recognised that the colonialist system was an anachronism which should no longer be allowed to exist, many people wondered whether the MPLA would be able to fulfil the task it had shouldered or whether it would prove to be a flash in the pan which would vanish leaving behind only a manifesto.

Life showed that the MPLA fulfilled the task it had set itself.

And when on the night of February 3, 1961 shooting broke out in the streets of Luanda, the capital of Angola, only a few people realised that it heralded the beginning of a drawn-out national liberation war. In February 1961 the London newspaper *The People* wrote that the uprising in the colony was a blow at Salazar's dictatorship. It pointed out that according to reports heavily censored by the Salazar authorities, the uprising had been crushed. But *The People* was wrong. The uprising was not crushed and February 4, 1961 marked the beginning of the armed struggle of the Angolans against the colonialists, the beginning of a long battle which lasted fourteen years.

The MPLA with its armed forces fought not only against Salazar's fascist regime. It also had to fight against the circles which overtly assisted the Portuguese colonialists throughout the long years of the war in Angola. These circles gave fascist Portugal diplomatic and political assistance and supplied Salazar's army with weapons and ammunition and since they held command positions in industry and agriculture not only in Portugal but also in her colony, they had very close economic links with the Lisbon regime.

I shall endeavour to prove this on the basis of concrete examples. First, their diplomatic assistance.

* * *

The year 1960. It has gone down in the history of mankind as Africa Year. In 1960 seventeen independent states emerged on the African continent. In 1960 the UN General Assembly examined the Soviet draft declaration on the final liquidation of colonialism. On December 14 delegations from 86 countries, including the Soviet Union, voted for the Declaration on the Granting of Independence to Colonial Countries and Peoples. The United States refused to support the declaration and acted in a bloc with Salazar's Portugal and the racialists of the Union of South Africa.

Two years passed. In that period more African states achieved independence. The struggle for independence launched in February 1961 in Angola under MPLA leadership continued. Le Partido Africano da Independencia da Guinée e Cabo Verde (PAIGC) energetically prepared for the struggle for the liberation of "Portuguese" Guinea. On November 27, 1961 a Special UN Committee for Decolonisation (Special Committee on the Implementation of the Declaration on the Granting of Independence to Colonial Countries and Peoples) began to function. One of its 17 members was the United States whose subsequent actions showed that it joined the Committee for the sole purpose of hampering its work.

The year 1962. The Seventeenth Session of the UN General Assembly. The Soviet Union proposed that the General Assembly should demand immediate independence for the colonies. The US voted against this proposal.

The year 1963. The Eighteenth Session of the UN General Assembly. It adopted a resolution prohibiting delivery of weapons to South African racialists. The United States voted against.

The year 1965. On May 4 the Special Committee adopted a decision to hold its session in three African countries to give representatives of national liberation movements a chance to address its sittings. The United States voted against.

A few days earlier MPLA Chairman Agostinho Neto gave an interview to a *Pravda* correspondent in which he said: "I would like through the *Pravda* newspaper which always comes out on the side of the liberation struggle of the Angolan people to express our warm gratitude to the Soviet people for their lofty internationalist sentiments. However great the distance between us we are always aware of their solidarity and support."

The Twentieth Session of the UN General Assembly which opened in September of that year confirmed the ban on all assistance to Salazar's Portugal and the Republic of South Africa. The United States voted against the imposition of this ban.

Early in 1966 the CPSU held its 23rd Congress. In his report General Secretary of the CPSU Central Committee L. I. Brezhnev referred to the national liberation movements and colonialism and said in part: "In Angola and Mozambique, in 'Portuguese' Guinea ... patriots are heroically fighting the foreign enslavers and invaders. ... Our Party and the entire Soviet people actively support this struggle; we are giving effective all-round assistance to peoples fighting against foreign invaders for freedom and independence and shall continue to do so. We are firmly convinced that the day is not far distant when the last remnants of colonialism will be destroyed and the people will raise the banner of national freedom in the liberated territories."

Several months later, on June 22, 1966 the Special UN Committee for Decolonisation held another session in Algiers. It adopted three resolutions one of which concerned the Portuguese colonies and contained the following lines: "The Special Committee ... reaffirms the inalienable right of the peoples of the African Territories under Portuguese domination to freedom ... and recognises the legitimacy of their struggle to achieve this right. .. , condemns the colonial policy of Portugal and its persistent refusal to carry out the resolutions of the General Assembly and the Security Council [on the granting of independence to colonial countries and peoples–Ed.]", and "appeals to all states to give the people of the Territories under Portuguese domination the moral and material support" they needed. Only one delegation, that of the United States, voted against the resolution and thus confirmed its solidarity with Salazar's Portugal. The Twenty-First Session of the UN General Assembly which was held the same year adopted a resolution condemning Portugal for waging colonial wars against the peoples of Angola, Mozambique and 'Portuguese' Guinea. The United States voted against this resolution.

The year 1967. The Twenty-Second Session of the UN General Assembly. It examined the implementation of the

1960 Declaration on Colonialism and passed a resolution condemning Portugal's colonial war against the peoples of Angola and Mozambique and appealed to the Portuguese Government to grant the peoples of the Portuguese colonies an opportunity to exercise their right to self-determination. The Soviet Union with an overwhelming majority of delegations voted for this resolution, but the United States refused to sign it and once again sided with fascist Portugal and the South African racialists.

The year 1968. The Twenty-Third Session of the UN General Assembly. It adopted a resolution in which 85 countries condemned the Portuguese colonialists for refusing to implement the Declaration on the Granting of Independence to the Colonial Countries and Peoples. Eighty-five delegations appealed to all countries and peoples to furnish moral and material assistance to the peoples of Angola, Mozambique and other Portuguese colonies in their struggle for liberation.

The Soviet Union voted for this resolution; the United States did not.

At the same session the USSR tabled a resolution condemning the employment of mercenaries to suppress national liberation movements. The US delegation voted against, thus approving the employment of hired assassins in Africa.

The year 1969. The Twenty-Fourth Session of the UN General Assembly. Once again its agenda included questions of decolonisation. It condemned the foreign monopolies which exploited the population and the national resources of the colonial territories, appealed to international organisations to render every assistance to the peoples fighting for independence, and confirmed the inalienable right of the peoples of Angola, Mozambique and 'Portuguese' Guinea to self-determination and independence. The Soviet Union voted for all these resolutions. The United States did not.

The same year the Security Council on three different occasions examined acts of aggression committed by fascist Portugal's armed forces against Zambia, Senegal and the Republic of Guinea. And each time the US representative on the Council did not cast his vote to condemn Portugal's aggression and thus refused to support the African countries.

The year 1970. The tenth anniversary of the adoption of the Declaration on the Granting of Independence to Colonial Countries and Peoples. Some months prior to the opening of the Twenty-Fifth anniversary session of the United Nations, a very representative international forum—Conference of Solidarity with the Struggle of the Peoples of the Portuguese Colonies—gathered in the Italian capital with delegates from 64 countries representing 171 national and international organisations attending. Angola was represented by a delegation led by MPLA Chairman Agostinho Neto. A delegation of the Soviet Afro-Asian Solidarity Committee attended the forum in behalf of the USSR.

After the conference the *Pravda* on July 5, 1970 published an interview with the Vice-Chairman of the Soviet Solidarity Committee, Corresponding Member of the USSR Academy of Sciences V. Solodovnikov. "The Soviet Union," he said, "supports the armed struggle of the patriotic organisations of the Portuguese colonies. It sends them weapons, transport and communications facilities, clothing and other commodities and equipment essential for waging a successful struggle against the colonialists. We also ship food and manufactured goods to the population of the liberated areas of these countries. Military and civilian specialists are being trained in the USSR." Five and a half years later, on January 3, 1976, the *Pravda* in one of its regular articles on Angola wrote: "The Soviet Union makes no secret of the fact that it has furnished and is furnishing moral and material aid to the patriotic forces of Angola, the Popular Movement for the Liberation of Angola (MPLA) in their struggle against colonialism." Thus the Soviet Union consistently fulfilled and continues to fulfil its internationalist duty.

On December 12, 1970 the UN General Assembly endorsed a programme of action designed to ensure the full implementation of the 1960 Declaration. The programme qualified as criminal the preservation of colonialism, and confirmed the inalienable right of the colonial peoples to fight with all the means at their disposal against the colonial powers which suppressed their aspiration to freedom and independence. It called upon the UN member-states to promote effective measures aimed at securing the complete implementation of the Declaration. Naturally the Soviet Union unconditionally supported this programme, but the United States voted against it.

In the spring of 1971 the 24th Congress of the Communist Party of the Soviet Union adopted the historic Peace Programme whose fifth point proclaimed: "The UN decisions on the abolition of the remaining colonial regimes must be fully carried out. Manifestations of racism and apartheid must be universally condemned and boycotted." The CC Report to the Congress made the following point: ". . .We declare that, while consistently pursuing its policy of peace and friendship among nations, the Soviet Union will continue to conduct a resolute struggle against imperialism, and firmly to rebuff the evil designs and subversions of aggressors. As in the past, we shall give undeviating support to the people's struggle for democracy, national liberation and socialism."

Among the guests at the Congress was an MPLA delegation led by its Chairman Agostinho Neto. "In the ten years of revolutionary struggle," he told the Congress, "our movement, our people and our fighters who comprise the advance detachment of Angola's anti-colonial struggle, have come to know the friendship and support of the Soviet Union. We regard the Communist Party of the Soviet Union as one of the most important forces upon which we rely in the development of our liberation struggle."

In 1971 the UN General Assembly held its Twenty-Sixth Session. On December 10 the Assembly by 105 votes condemned the refusal of fascist Portugal to implement the Declaration on the Granting of Independence to Colonial Countries and Peoples and her colonial war against the peoples of Angola, Mozambique and Guinea-Bissau. It appealed to all states, particularly NATO members, to terminate all assistance which made it possible for Portugal to continue her colonial war. The Soviet Union vigorously supported the resolution while the United States, acting hand in glove with the Republic of South Africa and fascist Portugal, voted against. Likewise in 1971 the United States demonstratively withdrew from the UN Committee for Decolonisation.

In 1972 the Twenty-Seventh Session of the UN General Assembly passed a very important decision confirming that the national liberation movements—MPLA in Angola, FRELIMO in Mozambique and PAIGC in Guinea-Bissau—reflected the aspirations of the peoples of these countries and were their legitimate representatives. The General Assembly called on the governments of the UN member-states, non-governmental and other international organisations to solve all questions concerning these territories with the participation of representatives of their national liberation movements and extend all moral and material support for their struggle. It summoned all states and particularly those members of

NATO which continued to furnish assistance enabling Portugal to continue her colonial wars, to stop doing so. The USSR supported this resolution while the USA voted against it.

The year 1973. The Twenty-Eighth UN General Assembly. Once again the question of colonialism was on the agenda of the session and once again the General Assembly condemned the wars waged by the Caetano regime against the peoples of Angola and Mozambique and the aggression of the Portuguese armed forces against the peoples of the Republic of Guinea-Bissau. It demanded a stop to the deliveries of weapons and other military equipment which enabled Portugal to conduct colonial wars. The resolution was endorsed by 101 delegations, but again the United States with the South African racists voted against. It will be recalled that this took place a few months prior to the overthrow of the fascist regime in Portugal, so that virtually on the eve of the collapse of the Caetano regime the United States yet again came out in the UN in defence of the colonialists.

Chapter I, Article 2, Paragraph 5 of the Charter of the United Nations which also bears the signature of the United States reads: "All Members shall give the United Nations every assistance in any action it takes in accordance with the present Charter, and shall refrain from giving assistance to any state against which the United Nations is taking preventive or enforcement action."

The history of the discussion in the UN of the struggle of the peoples of the Portuguese colonies shows that while the Soviet Union in fulfilment of the UN Charter and the adopted resolutions consistently and undeviatingly supported the just struggle of the people of Angola and other Portuguese colonies, the United States inevitably sided with the colonialists, the sworn enemies of the peoples fighting for freedom and independence.

I have quoted resolutions, declarations and other documents adopted at various conferences, congresses, meetings and assemblies, particularly resolutions endorsed by the majority of UN members, showing how the US policy of "anti-colonialism" manifested itself in the period from 1960—Africa Year—right up to 1974 when fascism was overthrown in Portugal.

Instead of drawing conclusions let us cite two more quotations.

The first is from an article published on January 3, 1976 in the *Pravda,* organ of the Central Committee of the Communist Party of the Soviet Union, which spoke of Soviet assistance to the MPLA. "Such actions," it emphasised, "are fully consistent with the well-known decisions on decolonisation adopted by the United Nations and also the Organisation of African Unity."

The second quotation is from an article by Cyrus Sulzberger carried by *The New York Times* on December 27, 1975: "United States policy toward the African continent is emotionally influenced by two historical legacies. The first is a tradition of anticolonialism, dating from our own revolutionary origins.... President Lyndon Johnson told me (1967): 'There is a deep connection between our foreign policy in Africa and our internal policy on civil rights.'"

I do not intend to examine US internal policy on civil rights in this book. But as regards the assertion concerning the "tradition of anticolonialism" in the US, the opinion of the world public on this score differs from that entertained by journalist Cyrus Sulzberger. In order to become convinced of this one needs only to recall the discussion of the colonial question in the UN.

I have outlined the US stand in international organisations on the question of colonialism but I would like to add that the line of behaviour of the other colonial and former colonial powers such as Britain, France and the FRG differed but little from that of the United States.

I have shown the position of the imperialist powers on the example of the United States simply because it claims to be the leader of the western world.

The above facts prove that the imperialist powers did give Portugal their diplomatic support. Let us take a look now at their military assistance to the colonial army of Salazar and Caetano.

The year 1961. Fifty Sabre fighter aircraft were sent to Portugal within the framework of US military aid. The same year, in connection with the commencement of military operations in Angola NATO agreed that Portugal's contingent in this organisation should be reduced to one division. US military advisers began to train the Portuguese Army and according to Portuguese deserters in Angola, the accent was on anti-guerrilla warfare.

On May 8, 1961 Portuguese Foreign Minister Franco Nogueira told a conference of NATO ministers in Oslo that Portugal was entitled to use NATO military equipment in Angola just as France had used it in Algeria. The Portuguese journal *Revista de Marinha* summed up Portugal's contribution to NATO, which it could have forfeited if Portugal withdrew from it, as follows: bases ensuring the best communications between the European zone and the United States; the utilisation of bases in the Azores; supply bases on Madeira and the Cape Verde Islands; a guaranteed system of electronic and meteorological communications without which navigation on the seas and anti-submarine warfare would have been impossible in the event of war; availability of strategic materials such as uranium and tungsten and also products from the African provinces; defence of the mouth of the Congo. . . .

NATO Secretary-General Dirk Stikker, referring to the situation in Africa declared in Lisbon in October 1961: "We must unite against the Communist danger."

The same year the FRG granted Lisbon a loan of $40 million and two more loans totalling $50 million in the next two years.

In 1961, after the commencement of the national liberation war in Angola Britain delivered two frigates to Portugal, and before the year was out the press reported that they had been dispatched to "overseas territories".

1963. US Assistant Secretary of State for Africa Mennen G. Williams told a conference in Chicago that America was not interested in seeing the Portuguese withdraw from Africa or their influence decline in that continent.

In January 1963, the United States undertook to deliver thirty T–37C fighter aircraft to Portugal. In the same month an agreement was signed on extending the lease of bases on the Azores by the United States. In 1963, former Commander-in-Chief of NATO Armed Forces General Lyman Lemnitzer expressed admiration for the Portuguese colonial troops in the "overseas territories" where they were fighting not only in defence of principles, but also of raw materials and bases essential for the defence of Europe and the West as a whole.

In 1963 the US delivered thirty Cessna T-37C aircraft to Portugal.

In October 1963 the FRG and Portugal signed a military agreement under whose terms Portugal placed a military base in Beja at the disposal of the FRG in exchange for an undertaking to support the Portuguese war effort with all available means.

In 1965 Great Britain delivered 200 Austin jeeps to Portuguese Army.

In 1966 the English frigate *Dalrymple* was handed over to the Portuguese Navy. The same year the FRG delivered to Portugal forty Fiat G-91 (NATO R-4 type) fighter aircraft.

At the time, according to the Portuguese journal *Revista Militar* (1966) the Portuguese Army had British and French armoured personnel carriers, and French made Panhard vehicles with a 60-mm mortar and two 7.62-mm machine guns were delivered to "Portuguese" Guinea.

On August 4, 1967 the *Deutsche Tagespost* published an interview which Commander of the Portuguese Army in Angola General Hermès de Araùjo Oliveira granted a West German journalist. "It is clear," the general said, "that the Americans are determined to preserve the Portuguese provinces in Africa as a zone of peace.... The Portuguese General Staff has worked out methods of action in a modern guerrilla warfare which have been fully approved by American, French and British military critics. In this field we have drawn not only on the experience of French in Indochina and North Africa, but also on the experience of the German Abwehr in the struggle against the Resistance movements in France and Russia."

The same year, within the framework of NATO agreements, Portugal received M-41 and M-47 tanks and several hundred T-47 tanks.

In 1968, after Caetano had come to power, the United States and Portugal had talks on broadening the agreement on US bases in the Azores. According to the press reports the talks centred on the construction of bases for US Polaris submarines. In return the US was to deliver to Portugal military equipment valued at $200 million over the next five years. Reports to this effect were carried by *Newsweek, The Christian Science Monitor* and other publications. The same year US delivered the latest artillery weapons to Portugal to replace obsolete British and FRG weapons.

On April 22, 1969 the West German newspaper *Süddeutsche Zeitung* wrote: "Portugal's NATO allies, particularly the United States, are displaying increasing sympathy for her overseas policy."

In May 1969 the Portuguese journal *Revista de Marinha* reported that Portugal was to get three naval vessels equipped with helicopters and outfitted for long-term service in the "overseas territories" from the FRG.

Obviously, this list of military deliveries to Portugal by the NATO countries is far from complete. But the above facts show clearly enough that the Lisbon regime could wage wars against the national liberation movement for so many years only thanks to the aid from its NATO allies.

* * *

Now let us take a look at yet another aspect, economic, of the Angola issue.

At the end of 1975 the Committee on Decolonisation published a report at the UN headquarters. Analysing the activity of foreign corporations in the colonial territories its authors arrived at the conclusion that it reduced the territories "to the role of supplier of agricultural products and raw material to the metropolitan or other countries". Noting that foreign monopolies "earn high profits because of special privileges granted by the colonial administrations and the pursuance of a policy of racial discrimination. . ." and because "African labourers continue to receive wages several times lower than those of non-indigenous workers and have no social security benefits",, the report went on: "The high profits earned by the foreign monopolies continue to be taken out of the Territories or to remain in the hands of the exploitative minority of foreign settlers and are not used for improvement of the economic and social conditions of the colonial peoples."

These conclusions referred to all the colonial territories of southern Africa. But since we are concerned with Angola, we shall examine the situation which took shape there towards the end of 1973, several months prior to the collapse of the fascist regime in Portugal.

The third issue of the British *Quarterly Economic Review* for 1973 and its annual supplement described the economic situation in Angola and Mozambique. Here are some figures the review mentioned. The development of rich iron ore deposits was launched in Kassinga at the end of 1973, and the feasibility of exploiting deposits of magnetite, copper, phosphates, gypsum and uranium was being studied. Manganese deposits estimated at 80-100 million tons were discovered in Cabinda. The daily oil output reached 130,000 barrels by the end of 1971. The annual production of diamonds was over 1,500,000 carats. With the completion of a hydroelectric scheme on the Cunene River the production of electricity in Angola would reach 10,300 million kilowatt hours. Metallurgical enterprises have been built and the construction of a metallurgical enterprise in Luanda has been approved. The authorities intended to impose no taxes on investments into new industrial enterprises for a period of up to 18 years. High growth rates were registered at enterprises manufacturing plastic goods, chemicals, tobacco and also at food factories. The annual volume of railway freightage was drawing close to 10 million tons.

Such was the general picture of industrial development in Angola, a country twice the size of France, with a population of approximately six million. And even though only a small portion of Angola's natural wealth has been surveyed, the above facts show that she is an extremely rich country with a colossal potential. Who exploited Angola's wealth? Who owned the factories, mines, mills, railways, oilfields and enterprises of the processing industry listed in the *Quarterly Economic Review*?

I have before me an issue of the British *Labour Research* bulletin. Here is an excerpt from one of its articles.

"British capital has a substantial stake in this impoverished country [Angola–O.I.]. Central to the entire economy is the Benguela railway which runs 838 miles from Lobito, Angola's main port, to the Katanga province of the Congo. The Benguela railway is the Katanga's main line with the outside world, and a large proportion of the output of Union Miniere du Haut Katanga, which virtually controls the Katanga copper belt, is transported to Lobito and shipped from there. Needless to say the Benguela railway is owned by Tanganyika Concessions, the British company with substantial minority interests in Union Miniere." Mentioning that captain Charles Waterhouse, a former Tory M. P., was chairman of Tanganyika Concessions (Tanks), the article went on to say: "Among the directors of the Benguela railway are the Earl of Selborne (Conservative peer, member of the Council of the Economic League) and Sir Ulick Alexander, who has been keeper of the Privy Purse to the Queen since 1952. Both these men are also directors of 'Tanks' and of Union Miniere.

"The Angola Diamond Company has the sole rights over about 390,000 square miles. In addition to diamond mining it has agricultural, industrial and financial interests in Angola. The company is incorporated in Portugal, and the Angola Government has a minority shareholding. There are two South African directors from De Beers on the company—Mr. Harry Oppenheimer and Mr. Harry Joel.

"Another British company, Angola Holdings, has a main interest in Companhia de Combustiveis which owns a bulk oil installation at Lobito and is concerned in a search for oil along coastal plains of Angola. Linked with Angola Holdings is Walford Lines shippers, which has a subsidiary in Angola.

"Hull, Blyth and Co., coal and oil contractors, ships agents, etc., also has a subsidiary in Angola. Among Hull, Blyth's directors is the Hon. F. A. Leathers, chairman of William Cory and Son ... son and heir to Viscount Leathers, Tory peer, and Minister of Transport during the War."

I selected this long quotation from an article which appeared in *Labour Research* in June 1961 at the time when the national liberation struggle had only just started in Angola and the Portuguese Government under Salazar very reluctantly permitted foreign capital investments into its "overseas territories". But even so, as can be seen from the quotation, foreign, at that time British, capital was already in control of the key branches of Angola's economy.

The penetration of foreign capital became particularly intensive after 1961 when the Portuguese Government flung Angola's doors wide open to it in order to finance Portugal's colonial wars. The Salazar regime granted numerous concessions to foreign investors allowing them to take up to 12 per cent of their profits on their investments out of the country. It should be noted that despite the growth of industrial production and mining, agriculture, in which foreign capital also played a leading role, remained the main branch of the Angolan economy. For example, Belgian capital held key positions in the production of such an important crop as coffee.

After 1961 US monopolies perceptibly strengthened their positions, particularly in the oil industry. Gulf Oil, a branch of the US Texaco company, controlled the oilfields of Cabinda. The second company, Petrangol, was a multinational corporation 28 per cent of whose shares were owned by General Mining, the Anglo-American Corporation and other South

African companies. The USA, the biggest consumer of Angolan oil, shipped out 50 per cent of the output.

The development of iron ore deposits estimated at 2,350 million tons near Kassinga was in the hands of the West German Krupp concern and two US concerns–Bethlehem Steel and General Electric. Subsequently, it was conducted with the financial participation of two other foreign companies–South African Industrial and Development Corporation and the Union Corporation.[1]

Thus, when the fascist regime in Portugal collapsed the overwhelming majority of key positions in the Angolan economy were in the hands of foreign monopolies. It should be noted, moreover, that in the last few years US capital managed to make considerable inroads not only at the expense of West German, French and Japanese but also British monopolies which until then held dominating positions in the Angolan economy. In the light of the above it would have been naive to think that foreign monopolies would stand idly by and leave it to the Angolans themselves to decide their country's future.

* * *

I have shown how western ruling circles, those of the United States in the first place, assisted Portugal in her war against national liberation movements. I have also endeavoured to define another important reason which induced the United States, Britain, France, Belgium and the FRG to make every effort to prevent patriotic forces in the Portuguese colonies, particularly Angola, from sweeping to victory, namely, their fear of losing the colossal profits they had amassed through the merciless exploitation of the natural wealth of these colonies.

Yet it would be wrong to think that western ruling circles failed to realise that the Portuguese would be compelled to withdraw from Africa one day and that the peoples of Guinea-Bissau, Mozambique and Angola would gain independence, either through armed struggle, or negotiations, or as a result of some sort of change in Portugal herself. In any case each passing day brought nearer the moment when the colonies would become independent states. So, as they sup-

---

[1] Henrique Guerra. *Angola. Estructura economica e classes socias*, Ed. Livrangol, 1975.

ported Portugal in the United Nations or dispatched yet another consignment of arms to Salazar's troops, Bonn, Paris and Washington devised long-term projects and plans to meet the events which were predetermined by the entire course of history—the forthcoming independence of the Portuguese colonies.

An account of one such project was given in the Johannesburg newspaper *The Star* on April 26, 1972 in an article by its Washington correspondent. The introduction to the article stated that the United States "set up the Southern African Student Programme, which set out to 'capture the revolution' in Southern Africa from the communists". Its purpose was "to educate in America exiled members of the African National Congress and the Pan-Africanist Congress who were likely leaders when the Whites were overthrown". Here are excerpts from the article: "Not many people in Washington know about the Southern African Student Programme, or SASP, as it is commonly called, but among those who do there is a fairly widespread belief that it is run by the Central Intelligence Agency through a double set of 'fronts'.

"The first is the State Department's Bureau of Cultural Affairs, which oversees its operation. The second is the outwardly respectable African-American Institute in New York.... Radical groups have named the African-American Institute and its monthly magazine *Africa Report,* as among the CIA front groups.... Ten years ago the United States ... set out to capture the future of Southern Africa by educating the men and women who were to govern when the Whites were overthrown. These rulers of the future numbering 519 so far, came from South Africa and South West Africa, from Mozambique and Angola and from Rhodesia.... As declared revolutionary exiles, they were America's investment in Southern Africa's future.... The official report of the African-American Institute gives this account of the origins of the programme: 'Although no one could predict how soon the wave of independence might reach into the south (of Africa), it was felt that training should be provided for Southern African refugee students who might eventually play a role in governing their home countries. In 1962 the Southern African Student Programme (SASP) was formed to provide US undergraduate study for students from Southern African countries.'

"...Mr. Damon Kletzien, who administers the SASP programme for the African-American Institute in New York... admits that the former Assistant Secretary of State for Africa Mr. G. Mennen Williams, presented it as a means of 'capturing the revolution' from the communists.... Incidentally, the official in charge of African Affairs at the State Department when the SASP programme was set up was Mr. Wayne Fredericks, whom ... Williams called his right-hand man. Oddly, Mr. Fredericks, now holding purse strings at the Ford Foundation, remains a major influence on the African-American Institute–which derives part of its funds from the Foundation–and therefore still close to the SASP programme...."

It should be noted that the American Government assigned approximately $10 million for the programme. True, a quarter of this sum went to cover the administrative costs of the African-American Institute. But the SASP and other similar programmes set up in a number of western countries yielded meagre dividends to their organisers. Damon Kletzien, for example, conceded that "in simple human terms, the results of the scheme to 'capture the revolution' have been pitiful...." This, however, does not apply to a number of other CIA operations which, fortunately for the peoples of Africa and particularly for the peoples of Angola, did end in complete failure in the long run but which, nevertheless, brought terrible suffering to hundreds of thousands of Angolans and caused enormous material damage to the country. We shall examine one such operation in the next chapter.

Chapter II

Jose Guilmore-
a CIA Agent

To begin with, here is a quotation from a special issue of *Tricontinental* journal published in Havana in 1975. "In 1878 the Baptist Missionary Society of London with the permission of the colonial Portuguese Government opened a mission in São Salvador, now capital of Zaire province in the north of Angola and the traditional capital of the Bakongo tribe. In 1885 the free state of the Congo was created which in 1908 became the Belgian Congo. . . .

"In 1955 Portugal installed a Catholic as tribal chief in São Salvador and Bakongo protestants emigrated to Leopoldville, capital of the then Belgian Congo. When the Portuguese-Catholic Bakongo chief died in 1957, the Bakongo protestants in Leopoldville set up their own organisation. It was established not for the purpose of liberating Angola and the Belgian Congo, but only in order to install their own man on the vacated throne of chief of the Bakongo in São Salvador. In November of that year they founded the Union of the Populations of North Angola (UPNA) with Manuel Barros Necaca, a friend of the Rev. George Hauser, Director of the American Committee on Africa (ACOA), as its president."

In its No. 10 issue in 1970 the Swedish information bulletin *Södra Africa* characterised UPNA as follows: "According to Marcum [*The Angolan Revolution: The Anatomy of an Explosion (1950-1962)* published by the MIT Press in 1969.–*Ed.*] UPNA was formed in close collaboration with the American Committee on Africa, ACOA, which was used by USA for its 'anti-colonial' offensive in Africa. UPNA did not want to be an Angolan liberation movement. This is shown by the fact that its president in 1957 wrote to the UN requesting that the Kingdom of Congo (in Northern Angola) should be restored." Taking all this into account the journal concluded that:

—the movement was regionally bound, or rather tribal, as it was to comprise only one tribe: Bakongo.

—the movement was formed outside Angola by politicians who had lived a long time in exile; people who had lost contact with their native country and who had established themselves in petty trade and bureaucracy in a foreign country.

—the movement was from the beginning connected with US interests through ACOA and its director George Hauser.

— the movement was monarchist, i.e., it aimed at preserving the system of chiefs instead of destroying it.

—the movement was reformist, i.e., it aimed at achieving independence by negotiations or international pressures.

But Manuel Barros Necaca died a few months after the formation of UPNA, and its leadership decided to hand over the reins of leadership in the organisation to Necaca's nephew, the thirty-year-old Jose Guilmore. Naturally, UPNA did not change its aim, that of creating a Kingdom of Congo in which the dominating role would be played by the elite of the Bakongo tribe.

Jose Guilmore was born in Angola but when he was only two years old his parents moved to the Belgian Congo and settled in Leopoldville. Several years later, on the advice of his uncle Manuel Barros Necaca, Guilmore was placed in a British protestant mission where he received an education. Upon finishing school he got a job first with a Belgian financial department and then went to work for Concorde—an insurance company in Stanleyville. In that period he made the acquaintance of Congo's future political leaders, including the Chairman of the National Movement of the Congo Cyrille Adoula and former chief of the Bakongo tribe Kasavubu. Subsequently both men earned notoriety by becoming zealous myrmidons of the US colonialists.

For a while Jose Guilmore dreamt of a day when he would ascend the throne in São Salvador to reign over the whole ancient kingdom of Congo. But these were only dreams for the throne was occupied by a Catholic king whom the Portuguese had installed in the royal palace in São Salvador. So Jose Guilmore decided to act. He knocked together a group of conspirators, supplied them with money and sent them on a secret assignment to São Salvador. The purpose of their mission became known in 1957 when the Catholic king of the Bakongo tribe Antonio III was poisoned. But while the king was removed without too much difficulty it was not at all simple to take his place. The Portuguese authorities would have refused to install a person from the Belgian Congo as the head of the Bakongo tribe which lived on Angolan territory. So UPNA President Jose Guilmore sent a letter to the UN requesting assistance in the restoration of the Kingdom of Congo. Some time later, however, he temporarily put aside his monarchistic aspirations. At least one can draw this conclusion from his letter in 1958 to the US, this time addressed to ACOA Director George Hauser, a friend of Guilmore's deceased uncle, which contained the following sentence: "The problems of the recreation of the ancient Kingdom of Congo will be raised later when circumstances permit to do so."

Thus, on the one hand, Guilmore knew that he would be unable to ascend the coveted royal throne in São Salvador, but, on the other, having been installed as UPNA President he was no longer satisfied with this modest position of bookkeeper at an insurance company. His acquaintance with Kasavubu and Adoula gave him the idea of fully dedicating himself to "political activity" which he regarded as a lucrative occupation. Characterising Jose Guilmore the British journalist Antonio de Figueiredo quoted Jonas Savimbi who had once collaborated with the former, as saying that Guilmore "saw Angola more as a big business than a patriotic cause". At the time serious changes were ripening on the African continent. National liberation movements were gathering momentum in British, French, Belgian and Portuguese colonies and the ruling circles in the colonial powers were aware that their undivided rule in Africa was coming to an end. Jose Guilmore decided to capitalise on the situation and do a bit of fishing in muddy waters. He went to Kasavubu who through Adoula managed to get him a Congolese passport in the name of Rui Ventura. Under this name Guilmore appeared in Accra where with a letter of recommendation to Kwame Nkrumah which he obtained in Leopoldville, he visited the Ghanaian President who promptly attached him to the African Department of the Ghanaian Foreign Ministry. Very quickly Guilmore wormed his way into the confidence of the President's personal adviser Georges Padmore. This was early in November 1958, shortly before the First All-African Peoples' Conference which took place in Accra from December 8 to 13. Invitations were sent to the majority of the continent's nationalist organisations and one was presented in Accra to Jose Guilmore as UPNA "president".

On December 8 thousands of Accrans welcomed the delegates and guests as they proceeded to a building near the ocean coast where the All-African Peoples' Conference was about to begin. The conference hall was decorated with slogans reading "Forward towards independence", "Colonialists, hands off Africa", "Africa must be free". More than 300 delegates representing 50 organisations from 28 · African countries, of which only 10 were independent, arrived for the conference.

Seated in one of the rows was a lean man. His lips were closed tight and his eyes were hidden behind a pair of sunglasses. He was Jose Guilmore, UPNA "president". He listened attentively to the speeches and during the break in the proceedings tried to get as close as possible to Sékou Touré of Guinea who was in the centre of attention as leader of a delegation of what was at the time the youngest independent country in Africa. The Republic of Guinea had been proclaimed just two months earlier, in the first days of October, and it was expected that the session of the UN General Assembly underway in New York would accept it to full UN membership.

Jose Guilmore decided to make the most of the favourable situation to build up political publicity for himself. And so one day he circulated a statement at the conference announcing that henceforth the Union of the Populations of North Angola (UPNA) would be called the Union of the Populations of Angola (UPA). It was a move which enabled Guilmore with a flourish of the pen to turn his tribalistic organisation, which acted only in behalf of the Bakongo tribe into a national organisation allegedly representing the entire population of Angola.

Prior to his departure from Leopoldville for Accra Guilmore had received a letter from his benefactor, ACOA Director George Hauser. It was a reply to the letter containing Guilmore's plans for recreating the Kingdom of Congo. Hauser informed Guilmore that he could help him in some respects but it was essential for Guilmore to come to New York.

This was easier said than done. Where could he get the money for the trip to New York? Moreover, the United States granted entrance visas only to persons holding a passport of an independent African country. So that was another problem. At first glance, the situation seemed hopeless. But it was with good reason that Jose Guilmore tried to attract Sékou Touré's attention and show himself in the best possible light. Eventually he crept into the good graces of the Guinean representatives and when the conference closed on December 13 and its delegates began to leave hospitable Accra, the Guinean delegation flew to Conakry taking along the former "president" of UPNA, now "president" of UPA Jose Guilmore. He gave Sékou Touré to understand that he would not mind working in Conakry for a time, provided, of course, that he could be useful to the Republic of Guinea. At the time this young state experienced an acute shortage of trained personnel. The French officials, specialists, engineers, technicians and bank employees were leaving Guinea after the proclamation of independence, and each more or less educated person was worth his weight in gold. Evidently, the Guinean delegation took this into consideration when they considered the question of whether they should or should not take Jose Guilmore with them.

In Conakry Guilmore realised that he made a very correct step. President Sékou Touré evinced the greatest sympathy for all those who wanted to fight for African independence. True, alongside honest people who were prepared to dedicate their strength and even their lives to the righteous cause, there was a fairly large number of adventurers, demagogues and ordinary reprobates who hastened to call themselves fighters for national liberation in the hope of deriving personal benefit. Later on all this scum would show their true face, but in that period they lost no time in capitalising on the situation. And Guilmore managed to gain the confidence of Sékou Touré, President of the Republic of Guinea.

As a result, in September 1959 the Guinean Mission in New York acquired a new staff member with a diplomatic passport. He was Jose Guilmore who shortly afterwards addressed one of the UN committees in behalf ... of the people of Angola.

On October 26 President of the Republic of Guinea Sékou Touré arrived in the United States on an official visit. He went to several cities and on November 5 addressed the UN General Assembly. The Guinean permanent representative at the United Nations in conversation with President Sékou

Touré commended the work of the Mission's new member Jose Guilmore without even suspecting that the latter had already been recruited by the US Central Intelligence Agency.

It happened on Sunday, October 25, 1959. Two men, an American and an African wearing dark glasses, were seated at a table in the restaurant of Hotel Tudor. They spoke in French.

"Mr. Guilmore," the American said, "Director of the American Committee on Africa, Mr. George Hauser, has a very high opinion of your activity. But you should realise that without our support you won't be able to make further progress. We'll help you to set up a real organisation and give you money and people. In all likelihood the Belgian Congo will soon become an independent state and, of course, we'll have an embassy there. You should take up residence in Leopoldville since there is nothing you can do in Conakry."

"But I'm with the diplomatic service of the Guinean Republic and Sékou Touré pays me a salary. On what will I live in Leopoldville?"

"We'll pay you a hundred dollars a month. I know that it's not a great deal of money and, of course, not enough to live on here, in New York or Washington. But there's a favourable rate of exchange in Leopoldville. Conditions are also different there so that you'll manage to make ends meet, but then everything will depend on your abilities and dedication. Don't forget that a hundred dollars a month is only a beginning, and our remuneration will depend on the results of your work. We're not against Angola becoming independent, but only some time in the future, naturally. Sooner or later the Portuguese will grant Angolans an autonomy of sorts, perhaps a federation and local self-government, and we, as the biggest power in the free world, want to see law and order preserved in Angola so that the country will flourish and not turn into a hotbed of international communism. I believe that in this respect our aims coincide."

"Yes, of course. But we have a problem here. As you know a number of organisations still exist in Africa which are working for the independence of Angola and one of them is the MPLA. Perhaps we should sound out Mario de Andrade[1] with the view to forming a united front?"

---

[1] Mario de Andrade was head of the MPLA, while Agostinho Neto was in prison at the time.—*Ed.*

"Under no circumstances. We look upon the MPLA as a communist organisation. It is supported by Russia and other communist countries. And it will be up to you to discredit the MPLA in the eyes of Africa and world public opinion. The MPLA will not decide the future of Angola. The US will see to that. And if you think that the UPA should act in alliance with the MPLA, then there is no reason to continue the conversation."

"I must have asked this question without thinking. I hoped that if we united with the MPLA the leading posts would be held by UPA members."

"You seem to forget, Mr. Guilmore, that so far your UPA is pure fiction. You have no programme, no clearly-defined political platform, no supporters, and most importantly, no money. But not so the MPLA which has plenty of everything, with the exception of money. It has ideas and programmes. So don't entertain vain hopes and don't try to enter into any alliance. You'll gain nothing and only stand to lose what you already have and what you may acquire in the future. Is that clear?"

"Yes."

The American pulled out a wallet from the side pocket of his jacket and extracted a small oblong envelope.

"Here is your remuneration for the current month. Although there are only six days left in October we are paying you the full sum, a hundred dollars, simply because we think well of you. Try to be at the American Committee on Africa tomorrow, Monday, at about six p.m. after you're through at the Mission. You know the address, it's 801 2nd Avenue. The Reverend George Hauser will give me the key from his office and I'll be waiting for you there. Your cooperation with us has to be finalised. It's a mere formality, of course, but financial departments like to have accounts in perfect order. You should know that I'm not paying you out of my own pocket."

"May I report my visit to the American Committee on Africa to my immediate superior? It is our duty to give an account of our movements and name the persons we meet. The head of the Mission keeps telling us to display maximum vigilance. If I'm seen talking with you I'll be in for a lot of trouble. I may even be expelled from the Mission and sent back to Conakry."

"You may report your visit to 2nd Avenue only when you

return to the Mission. But not a word before that. And if you don't keep quiet you'll be in such trouble that the order to return to Conakry will be a mere trifle in comparison. I'll remain here for a while. So don't forget, tomorrow at 6 p.m. in the ACOA offices."

The next day at about eight in the evening Jose Guilmore entered his New York apartment with a large yellow envelope stuffed with papers under his arm. Closing the door he took off his raincoat and sank back into a deep easy chair. For a few minutes he sat without moving, his eyes vacant, then he heaved himself from the chair and began pacing the room. Tiny hammers pounded in his temples. He went to the bathroom and splashed cold water on his face. He felt hot although it was fairly cool in the apartment.

Well, he had burned his bridges and was past the point of no return. Twisting his lips in a wry smile he recalled the meeting he had just had at the American Committee on Africa. So the contract was signed and he was on the payroll of the CIA and even listed under a special number. Strangely enough he could not remember it. To forget such an important thing. But what's the difference. Of course, he would not be the number one man in their game. But he would get his pay so long as they needed him, and that was the main thing.

He pulled out some booklets from his pocket. Two of them explained the aims and tasks of the American Committee on Africa. Of course there was nothing reprehensible in the activity of this organisation. One of the booklets said that the aim of the ACOA was "to interpret the meaning of African events to the American people; support policies which will further the development of responsible self-government in those parts of Africa where it does not exist; raise special funds in the United States to support projects in Africa to establish interracial cooperation, and oppose racial discrimination; and serve African people through African students in this country and through educational and service projects in Africa".

Guilmore threw the booklet on the table. Well written and absolutely above suspicion.

He went to the kitchen, poured himself a glass of orange juice, and making himself comfortable in the chair immersed himself in the booklets, some of which dealt with the activity of the Ford Foundation and others concentrated on the international links of the US labour unions. There were also a few copies of the *Africa Report* magazine. It would have been useful to make some sort of a summary of his conversation, he thought, but the American said that he was not to make any notes.

He rose to his feet, stretched his arms wearily and looked around the cosy sitting room. Soon he would be deprived of all this. Back in Africa it would be silly even to dream about such comfort. But, he recalled, the Americans promised him annual trips to the United States where, they decided, his organisation should have a bureau and its UPA staff would welcome him, Jose Guilmore, as their chief, as the president of a national liberation movement of the whole of Angola, a movement recognised by the United States. Not bad at all.

...The Permanent Representative of the Republic of Guinea to the United Nations was sincerely sorry when Guilmore said that he had decided to return to Guinea because his presence on the African continent was vital for the UPA. The leadership of the Guinean Democratic Party agreed with him and early in January 1960 he was back in Conakry. At the time a delegation of the Republic of Guinea was preparing to leave for Tunis to attend the Second All African Peoples' Conference, and Jose Guilmore was included too. There were four points on the agenda of the conference: the struggle for independence, neocolonialism and the struggle against it, the continent's social and economic development, and African unity. The leader of the Guinean delegation Abdoulaye Diallo performed the functions of General Secretary of the conference.

On January 23 delegates from many African countries assembled in the building of the Tunisian Labour Exchange. The centre of the city was festively attired. There were numerous posters with the emblem of the conference: a countour of the African continent capped with a torch with the slogan "Freedom and Unity" inscribed across the flame.

Opening the conference General Secretary Abdoulaye Diallo read out the list of delegates. At first he presented delegates from independent African countries, and then leaders of delegations sent by national liberation movements.

"We have the honour," Diallo declared, "to present delegations from the national liberation movements of Angola: Mario de Andrade, Lusio Lara and Viriato Cruz of the Movement for the Liberation of Angola, MPLA, and Holden Roberto of the Union of the Populations of Angola, UPA."

Jose Guilmore rose up, faced the hall and bowed. And so Jose Guilmore became Holden Roberto.

That was the name under which he began to operate in Africa. Under this name he was registered in the lists of CIA agents and under this name he became known to the world public when he undertook the dirty job of betraying the people of Angola.

The MPLA delegation had heard that there would be a UPA delegate at the conference. But knowing that this organisation pursued narrow tribalistic objectives and lacked the support of the Angolan masses, they did not attach too much significance to it. Still the MPLA delegation had been instructed to sound out the possibility of forming a united front with UPA, which, even if it had no influence in Angola as a whole, did have fairly strong links with the Bakongo tribe in the north of the country. Accordingly, one evening the MPLA delegation invited Jose Guilmore or Holden Roberto as he now preferred to be called, to a meeting at the hotel where the delegates to the conference were staying, to examine the possibility of forming a united front. Holden Roberto (henceforth we shall call Jose Guilmore only by that name) accepted the invitation. During the meeting with the MPLA he behaved in line with the instructions he had received from a member of the Central Intelligence Agency in the restaurant of Hotel Tudor in New York.

"I believe," he told the MPLA delegates, "that a merger of our organisations would be premature. Frankly speaking, your programme is unsuitable for myself and my friends, for my organisation, for UPA. Ours is a purely African organisation, while your MPLA includes mulattoes and white settlers. For whose freedom will we fight then? We're struggling against mulattoes, against the white settlers and against the Portuguese. We see no difference between them. African Negroes are much closer to us than Angolans with white skins, even if their grandfathers and fathers had been born in Angola. We shall fight against them, too. Our conversation, therefore, is pointless, and no matter how long we may sit here, I shall never consent to a merger."

Such was the outcome of the first attempt by the MPLA to form a united front with the UPA. Later, when they discussed Roberto's adamant stand, the MPLA delegation attributed it to his inadequate theoretical grounding and primitive, backward views unaware as yet that even if they were indisputable, these were third-rate factors and that the main cause was that Roberto was on the CIA payroll.

Back in Conakry Roberto, acting on the instructions he had received in New York asked the leadership of the Republic of Guinea for letters of recommendation to prominent functionaries of the national liberation movement in the Belgian Congo. Granting his request they sent a letter to Patrice Lumumba in Leopoldville in April 1960 asking him to support and help the UPA's leader Holden Roberto.

The proclamation of the independence of the Belgian Congo was scheduled for July 1. On June 29 Washington confirmed the appointment of Clare Hayes Timberlake as US Ambassador to the future independent African country. A few days after the proclamation of independence Holden Roberto flew to Leopoldville. There he vigorously sought to get acquainted with the new leaders of the Congo. A member of the US Embassy which had just been opened in the city advised him to get on friendly terms with Victor Nendaka who was in charge of security in the Lumumba government and also with Kandolo (Lopepe) and Mobutu. His relations with the latter two became particularly close. From the very outset the political situation in the independent Congo was extremely unstable and events were taking a grim turn. The imperialist circles were not inclined to lose such a rich region of Africa. The government headed by Patrice Lumumba did not suit them. The country's former masters, the Belgians, relying on all-round US support hatched plots designed at whatever the cost to remove patriotic-minded Congolese, in the first place Patrice Lumumba and his friends, from power. In the beginning of 1961 Patrice Lumumba was assassinated.

Recalling that period MPLA Chairman Agostinho Neto wrote in the beginning of 1964:

"...The Angolan nationalists always placed great hopes on independent Congo which would serve as an open gateway for supplying the Angolan national liberation movement with materials. The presence of half a million Angolans in the Congo (Leopoldville) was in itself an important reserve of forces which could be used as a rearguard of the movement unfolding in Angola.

"The chaos which broke out in the Congo shortly after the proclamation of independence gave the imperialists a much freer hand in the country which tried to use certain Congo-based Angolan organisations as a leading force in the struggle against the people of Angola.

"It is in this light that we should view the Adoula-Roberto coalition, and systematic obstruction by the Adoula government of any activity of the Movement for the Liberation of Angola (MPLA)."

While fulfilling various assignments for the members of the US Embassy (among other things he acted as a liaison agent between Kandolo and the US Ambassador Timberlake), Roberto hastened to establish the central organs of his organisation, for practically the entire UPA existed only on paper. A few months later he announced the composition of the UPA steering committee. Sixteen of its nineteen members were natives of the northeast of Angola and belonged to the Bakongo tribe. To be on the safe side he gave the main posts to his relatives:

John Edouard Pinock, UPA adviser, Holden Roberto's cousin;

Sebastião Roberto, deputy political chief, Holden's brother;

Johny Edouard Pinock, chief of information and the press, John Edouard Pinock's son;

Jos Peterson, head of the administration and security chief, Holden's brother-in-law;

Narciso Nekaka, secretary for propaganda, Holden's uncle;

Simão de Freitas, secretary of the women's movement and deputy security chief, Holden's cousin;

Eduardo Vieira Macenda, deputy secretary for the trade union movement, Holden's nephew.

Thus, seven members of the UPA steering committee were Holden Roberto's relatives.

He also strengthened his ties with Zaire by divorcing his first wife who belonged to the Bakongo tribe and marrying President Mobutu's cousin.

On February 4, 1961, an MPLA-led uprising broke out in Luanda. News of the events in the Angolan capital stirred world public opinion and meetings in support of the struggle of the Angolan people were held in various countries. Roberto's American bosses fearing that the organisation which they were supporting might disappear without having done anything at all to justify its existence, demanded that Roberto should make some sort of a move to wrest the initiative from the MPLA. Obedient to the will of his masters Roberto used his connections with people who had seized power in the Congo after the assassination of Patrice Lumumba, to launch a propaganda campaign over Leopoldville radio. He proclaimed himself a "messiah" whose mission was to liberate the Bakongo people from the domination of the whites. In his tape-recorded preachings over Leopoldville radio the "messiah" urged to "kill all whites and mestizos".

Early in March Holden Roberto flew to New York. Before departing he ordered his subordinates to start acting on March 15. The date was not chosen arbitrarily because on March 15, 1961 the UN Security Council was scheduled to meet in New York to discuss the situation in Angola. The UPA operation began on the Fazenda da Primavera plantation in the vicinity of São Salvador.

Recalling the events of those days journalist John Blair wrote in *The Guardian* almost 15 years later: ". . . There can be no doubt that Mr. Roberto and his organisation have a reputation for brutality, tribalism, and ritual mutilation of prisoners dating as far back as 1961. In March of that year thousands of Roberto's Bakongo tribesmen rose up against the Portuguese farmers and settlers in Northern Angola and while no accurate figures will ever be known, it is estimated that at least 750 Portuguese lost their live in the first three months of fighting. Their killing was characterised by . . . brutality. . . ."

The Portuguese Army conducted punitive operations against the peasants who, virtually unarmed, tried to assault Portuguese garrisons. Heedful of Roberto's preachings they sincerely believed that bullets and shells could not harm them and fell in their thousands from the fire of the Portuguese soldiers.

Returning from New York Roberto was summoned to the US Embassy. There he was taken over the coals for the "idiotic actions". In no uncertain terms he was told not to display initiative, and given instructions which he was to follow to the letter. Its central point was that the main objective of the UPA armed groups which cross from the Congo into Angola was to operate against MPLA detachments. He was also informed that weapons and ammunition for these operations would be placed at his disposal before long. The Leopoldville government was expected to turn over to Roberto and his organisation one of the military camps near the Congolese capital.

Roberto began to fulfil his bosses' instructions with truly extraordinary zeal. His bands massacred the population of the villages in the northern part of Angola which supported the MPLA. With the permission and help from the Congolese Government he established a number of strongpoints for his groups on the Angolan border in order to prevent MPLA fighters from crossing into Angola.

Journalist Anibal Melo wrote in this connection: "The sole purpose of UPA activity in the area of military operations in the north of the country is to spread racialist and tribalistic theories in order to divide the working masses in the Resistance movement, help the colonial army to suppress the liberation movements and seize the administrative and commercial centres which were already controlled by the insurrectionists. Therefore," he continued, "we conclude that the UPA is a counter-revolutionary movement because it stopped fighting the enemy, Portuguese colonialism, and concentrated on sabotage with the view to preventing an intensification of the armed struggle, and also on terrorism against politicians and other organisations, and even against some of its own members who disagreed with its activity."

In the latter half of 1961 Roberto met Irving Brown, an AFL-CIO representative in Europe, in Leopoldville and had a long conversation with him.

A word about Irving Brown. In the mid-forties, while holding the official post as one of the leaders of the reactionary International Confederation of Free Trade Unions (ICFTU) he had a hand in organising an espionage network in Europe for the US intelligence. In the period between 1947 and 1951 he made several trips to Greece where he turned over dossiers on Greek patriots compiled by the US intelligence to the Greek fascists. General Secretary of the Greek General Confederation of Labour Theos wrote that in 1947 alone the Greek police arrested 500 democrats in Athens and Piraeus on Brown's direct reports and in 1950, on the basis of documents furnished by Brown they arrested 118 leaders of progressive trade unions, and eight of them were sentenced to death. Later Brown became an AFL-CIO representative in Europe. His activity, however, was not confined solely to the European continent. And when in the beginning of the sixties the US intelligence became seriously interested in

Africa, Brown was dispatched to that continent. During his meeting with Holden Roberto in Leopoldville he drew up a programme of action in the trade union sphere for him.

On Brown's advice, Roberto went to Tunisia where the Tunisian Government was putting a group of young people from the UPA through a course of military training. There Roberto met Ahmed Tlili, Secretary of the Tunisian trade unions and, on his recommendation, hired a Cuban counter-revolutionary and CIA agent Carlos Kassel as his adviser on trade union affairs.

Kassel drew up documents announcing the formation of Central League of Angolan Working People and sent them to the ICFTU which was controlled by Americans at the time as an application for membership. As a result Roberto was able to obtain material assistance from the AFL-CIO and, subsequently Irving Brown became personally concerned with maintaining contacts with him.

In 1962 the Congolese authorities placed a military camp in Kinkuzu at Roberto's disposal, making this decision after a meeting of the Leopoldville authorities with the head of the US mission in the city George McMurtrie Godley. On his orders Roberto signed contracts with people designated by Godley and the CIA. Thus, he signed a contract with the American named Muller who became his personal adviser. Prior to that he was a liaison adviser to Moise Tshombe. Roberto also hired another American, John Marcum, as his personal adviser. (In 1976 John Marcum headed the California University of Santa Cruz).

Roberto also engaged the American Charles Dorkins to organise communications at the Kinkuzu base.

On the advice of the US Embassy Roberto set up other organisations, a young people's and a women's, in order to establish contact with corresponding international organisations which were under US control. The Americans made it clear that in this way he could receive financial and other aid from various sources and make it easier for the US to finance his organisation.

Early in 1962 Holden Roberto performed yet another manoeuvre. Besides the UPA there were a number of small nationalist organisations in Leopoldville uniting Angolan refugees, such for example, as the Zombo Refugees Alliance which was subsequently transformed into the Democratic

37

Party of Angola (PDA). Holden Roberto came to terms with the leadership of this small tribalistic organisation and on March 27, 1962 it merged with the UPA, and together they formed what became known as the National Front for the Liberation of Angola (FNLA).

In Leopoldville on April 5, 1962 Holden Roberto announced the establishment of "a republican government of Angola in exile" (GRAE) and proclaimed himself as its head.

How the national liberation organisations in the Portuguese colonies reacted to the formation of GRAE may be judged from two reports, one from Rabat, the other from Conakry.

A France Press correspondent in Rabat reported on the same day that the Chairman of the Consultative Council of the Organisation of Nationalist Parties of the Portuguese Colonies (CONCP) with headquarters in Rabat issued a statement on April 5 characterising the Provisional Government of the Republic of Angola as a puppet and its creation as bluff in the interests of Portuguese colonialism. The leader of the "provisional government" Holden Roberto, the statement continued, was "fully isolated in Angola herself and also from revolutionary Africa".

The statement pointed out that the chief of staff of the "liberation army" Major Cassanga had turned his back on Roberto, accusing him of unleashing a fratricidal war in Northern Angola and ordering the annihilation of about 8,000 Angolans who did not share his racialist views. He also accused him of ordering the assassination of the commander-in-chief of his own army and then blamed the Portuguese Army for this crime in order to appropriate the money received from the fraternal countries to assist the struggle of the Angolan People.

The Chairman of the Consultative Council also added that General Secretary of the Central League of Angolan Working People Cacinda charged Roberto with embezzling funds received from the ICFTU.

On April 7, a France Press correspondent reported from Conakry that in a statement for the press the MPLA issued a warning, particularly to those African countries which may be led into error and recognise the Provisional Government of the Republic of Angola with Holden Roberto as Prime Minister. If they did so, the statement went on, these countries would have to bear the responsibility for perpetuating the split between Angolan nationalists. As regards the participation of the Democratic Party of Angola in this Provisional Government, the MPLA statement emphasised, that Party was in fact an alliance of representatives of the Zombo tribe, an ethnic minority in the Congo province. This manoeuvre was designed to isolate on the political arena the MPLA, which was regarded as too dangerous from the point of view of the ambitious plans of certain elements. The MPLA went on to say that it did not recognise the legality of the Provisional Government of the Republic of Angola because the way in which it had been formed and the source from which it had sprung clearly disclosed its anti-popular nature. This government would never be trusted and those countries which may recognise it would also forfeit the trust they had enjoyed. There was every reason to say, the statement added, that the existence of this so-called government discredited the struggle of the people of Angola.

The African countries did not hasten to recognise the self-styled government in spite of its intensive sales talk. Even a year after the formation of GRAE not a single African state announced its intention to establish official relations with the FNLA and its "government". Thereupon, acting on direct instructions from the US Ambassador Edmund Asbury Gullion, Holden Roberto organised trips for journalists, but only American, to FNLA bases on the border with Angola. Shortly afterwards the US press printed a series of articles praising GRAE "guerrilla detachments" and, naturally, Holden Roberto himself. A detailed account of these trips was given in *The New York Times*.

The year 1963 witnessed the establishment of the Organisation of African Unity (OAU). The events of that period were described in a Declaration issued by the Central Committee of the Democratic Party of Guinea on December 11, 1975:

"At the time of the establishment of the Organisation of African Unity we were a member of a group which in May 1963 submitted a draft resolution providing for assistance to liberation movements on the part of the independent states. We proposed that each African state should contribute a sum equal to one-tenth of its budget to a fund which would be raised to finance the activities of the liberation movements.... The proposed percentage was not approved by the majority which considered that each country should be given an opportunity to aid the liberation movements as it sees fit.

"On June 15, 1963 the Guinean National Assembly ratified the OAU Charter and the law on the ratification was published on June 18. The decision of the OAU was ratified and published also on June 15 and 18. This ratification authorised the President of the Republic to allocate 1 per cent of the national budget to the fund of assistance to African nationalists fighting for the independence of their countries. Thus, the Republic of Guinea was the first African state to offer practical proof of its adherence to the historic Charter of the OAU and translate into reality one of the first and most important resolutions of the continental organisations on the first day of its establishment.

"Our stand, which consisted in doing everything to furnish the liberation movements with concrete aid, led to the formation of the OAU Committee of Liberation and motivated some of our initiatives in favour of the nationalists such as Holden Roberto. . . .

"With our support, as we have already said, Holden Roberto asserted everywhere that he represented all those who were fighting in Angola. We must admit that we ourselves were misled. Thus, for example, on our initiative the OAU Committee of Liberation in July 1963 recognised GRAE, and Holden Roberto who was regarded as head of state could in this capacity participate in the OAU. The Kinshasa Government under Mobutu hastened to prohibit all MPLA activity on the territory of Zaire and closed the border between Zaire and Angola along its entire length. As a result a terrible blow was dealt to the liberation struggle in Angola."

Guided by the best of intentions the Republic of Guinea, which had been taken in by Roberto's rhetoric, did play a part in removing barriers to the recognition of GRAE by the OAU. But the decisive role in this respect was played by the backstage machinations of US Assistant Secretary of State for African Affairs Mennen G. Williams and the head of the so-called good offices mission Wachuku both of whom were in Leopoldville at the time.

Only one government recognised GRAE fifteen months after it had been established, and that was the Government of the Congo (Leopoldville) which made an announcement to this effect on June 29, 1963 in spite of the fact that the OAU advised its members not to hurry.[1] Confronted with a *fait accompli* the OAU Committee of Liberation decided to send a mission led by Wachuku to Leopoldville to study the situation on the spot. This is what Agostinho Neto wrote about the events which took place in Leopoldville in those days:

"Motives for Recognition

"The geographic and economic position of Angola lying in the zone of Southern Africa which Mr. Williams wants to unite into a new African community poses serious problems before the national liberation movements in the countries of that part of the continent. Is there any need to recall the talks which took place in June 1963 between Adoula and Williams, between Adoula and Wachuku and between Wachuku and Williams? One of their results was recognition of the FNLA as a provisional government and the publication of the statement announcing the establishment in Leopoldville of the House of National Liberation Movements of South Africa, Mozambique, Southwest Africa and Spanish Guinea.

"Are not these two facts elements of a broad strategic plan?

"It is ridiculous to say as some people do that recognition was extended to the FNLA government because the MPLA was allegedly weak. In actual fact this recognition came at the time when the imperialists and their agents in Leopoldville realised that in spite of the obstacles which they put in the path of the MPLA, they failed to prevent this party from strengthening its positions on all the fronts, a circumstance which tended to increase the scope of the uprising in Angola. The plans entertained by Adoula, who sought recognition for the FNLA as the only Angolan organisation which waged a struggle, were unmasked at the Conference of Heads of African States and Governments in Addis-Ababa. But the defeat in Addis-Ababa did not discourage FNLA's patrons.

---

[1] Here is an interesting fact. In the FNLA statement proclaiming the establishment of GRAE these letters were spelled out as Governo Respublicano Angolano no Exilo. But when this government was officially recognised in Leopoldville Congolese officials erred in deciphering the letter "R", and called it a revolutionary instead of a republican government. Holden Roberto promptly seized upon this slip and insisted that henceforth his government should be known only as Revolutionary Government of Angola in Exile–*(O. I.).*

"Just then US Assistant Secretary of State Mennen Williams arrived in Leopoldville and soon afterwards the Congo announced its recognition of the 'Angolan Government'. This was done without the knowledge of a number of ministers of the central Congolese Government.

"The OAU Committee of Liberation at its first sitting decided to dispatch a good offices mission to Leopoldville to find a way for averting the disastrous consequences of Adoula's unilateral decision.

"Led by Wachuku the good offices mission acted in a similar vein and, instead of working out a platform for the united actions of political parties, it turned into a tribunal determined to put an end to the MPLA. Without hearing out the MPLA leader it manipulated with procedural issues and without ever leaving the palace where it met it agreed with Adoula's and Roberto's arguments concerning FNLA's primacy. Not bothering to check the veracity of these arguments it declared itself competent to recommend the recognition of the so-called government which was hastily created under the patronage of an American diplomat.

"This mediation was detrimental to the peoples of Angola and contrary to the decisions of the Addis-Ababa Conference.

"...Now, nine months after the strange recommendations of the Committee of Liberation it will be expedient to sum up the activity of the group calling itself 'provisional government'.

"Statements, frequently contradictory and fantastic, which were made by FNLA representatives in the Congo, Egypt, the USA, Tunisia and Algeria show how premature and opportunistic the recognition of the 'government' of Angola was. Obviously, it was neither representative nor efficient. Yet its recognition poses difficult political issues today, and because this government serves imperialist interests it makes ineffective the assistance which is channelled to the people of Angola through this 'government'.

"The Angolan masses continue to demand unity of action on the part of political organisations. They want to know why the weapons which are delivered to the FNLA are not made available to them and why Adoula boycotts the MPLA guerrillas. The struggle has entered a stage when the patriots have to act all together and the MPLA works precisely in this direction proposing once again immediately to convene a congress of all nationalist organisations of Angola."

In February 1964 a new US Ambassador arrived in Leopoldville to replace Edmund Gullion. The new ambassador, George McMurtrie Godley was not exactly a newcomer in Leopoldville. He had already been there as deputy head of a US mission in 1962. Upon returning to the US he was placed in charge of the Office of Central African Affairs of the Department of State, and was closely associated with the CIA. His very appointment to Leopoldville indicated that US attached great significance to that part of the African continent.

At the end of March US Assistant Secretary of State Averell Harriman visited Leopoldville. There he attended a meeting organised by the head of the Congolese Government Adoula and then had a series of private talks with Holden Roberto. Also present was Roberto's former personal adviser John Marcum who had since become Harriman's adviser on Portuguese colonies. Following Harriman's departure from Leopoldville on March 31, the US Embassy set up a special section for Angolan affairs headed by Heatter and Devnis who maintained very close contacts with Holden Roberto. From that day Roberto took all his orders from this section. Carrying out Devnis's instructions Roberto in April 1964 hired Bernhardt Manhertz, an American officer who had served with the US Army in Vietnam, and placed him in charge of FNLA armed detachments. Incidentally, the Cuban counter-revolutionary Carlos Kassel had already returned to Leopoldville by then. After fulfilling his mission of organising the so-called Angolan trade unions and getting them into the ICFTU Kassel on Roberto's instructions had gone to Algiers with John Pinock. But when in 1963 Algeria was preparing to welcome Fidel Castro Kassel was ordered to leave the country and in 1964 he and Manhertz worked together under Roberto. Here is what was said about this period in an article in No. 6 *Afrique-Asie* journal published on December 24, 1973:

"In 1964 Holden Roberto contracted a veteran of the Vietnam war Bernhardt Manhertz to reorganise his armed forces. This American specialist in anti-guerrilla warfare in his turn hired Cuban anti-Castroite officers. This group was headed by one Carlos Kassel, an authority on trade unions who had been in the service of Battista and Trujillo. He was made commander of Roberto's detachments and placed in charge of external relations. After several months of intensive work the Manhertz-Kassel group managed to raise armed units which began to operate on the border between the Congo (Leopoldville) and Angola for the purpose of preventing MPLA groups from penetrating into Angola and Cabinda. . . . But this reorganisation which was carried out with the help of foreign specialists was not to the liking of some of Roberto's associates. In June 1965 Alexandre Taty, GRAE Minister of Armaments at the time who was engaged in blackmarketing a hundred tons of armaments delivered by one of the Maghreb states to Roberto, tried to organise a military coup and proclaimed the formation of a military junta which was to replace GRAE. But the attempt fell through thanks to swift interference by Kinshasa security forces which went into action on orders from the Adoula government. Thereupon Taty went over to the Portuguese and was made a colonel of the Portuguese occupation army."

After Taty's unsuccessful attempt to overthrow Roberto, the CIA decided to bolster the position of its agent. Here is an excerpt from a booklet entitled *How American Secret Agents Operate in Africa* which was published in 1967.

"In September 1965, a plane was revving up its engines on the concrete runway of the airport in Rochester (New York). The pilot—John Hauck, 28, a powerfully built man with black hair, was standing beside it engaged in conversation with two people. One of them was Australian–born Gregory Boord who sported moustache and had only recently received US citizenship, and the other was Count Henri Mari Français de Marin de Monmarin, a greying Frenchman with a military bearing.

"The plane's cargo mas unusual: bombs, arms and ammunition. When the customs official, surprised at such a cargo, asked the pilot whether he had the appropriate documents, Hauck's reply was quite unexpected—he merely said "Sparrow" and "Monarch". The amazed official reported this to his superiors who immediately ordered him to leave the pilot and his plane alone. The two words pronounced by Hauck were given him as passwords which could open any door and protect him from the curiosity of unauthorised persons.

"Both Hauck and other pilots . . . delivered planes to Angola . . . for various provocations in favour of Holden Roberto."

Of course, Roberto's close links both with the CIA and US embassies did not remain unnoticed and already in those years the world press often wrote about his contacts with spurious circles in the United States.

Here are several quotations drawn from different sources. In his book *Portugal in Africa* which was published in London in 1962, James Duffy wrote: "...No less an authority on international Communism than the Central Intelligence Agency reportedly made an investigation of the UPA and satisfied itself that it was an authentic African nationalist party free of any Communist association" (London, 1962, p. 218).

It will be recalled that the FNLA came into being in March 1962 following the merger of the UPA with the small tribalistic organisation DPA (Democratic Party of Angola). A few weeks earlier, on February 5, DPA Vice-President Matumona wrote in *Courier d'Afrique:* "Almost all material and financial assistance for the UPA comes from the United States or to be precise, from the American Committee on Africa. This financial assistance is furnished on condition that the UPA will not unite with MPLA forces or with any other front of which the MPLA might become a member."

Kweku Dadson in his *How American Secret Agents Operate in Africa* described Roberto in the following terms:

"...Having figured out that Holden Roberto is an ambitious and unscrupulous person, the Central Intelligence Agency decided to place its stake on him in the big game it was playing.

"In supporting Salazar in his attempts to suppress the nationalist movement in Angola, Mozambique and Portuguese Guinea the Americans realise full well that although historically this struggle is inevitable, it is a hopeless struggle for Portugal. Therefore, they are already taking measures to ensure their interests in these countries towards the day these countries gain their independence.

"These measures boil down to the following: first of all, to get the largest possible number of reliable people into the future governments, and, secondly, to get rid of all the leftist elements and leaders who will not adhere to a pro-American orientation and will align themselves with other foreign powers. And Holden Roberto was selected for this delicate mission.

"It cost the CIA considerable efforts and a lot of money to turn Holden Roberto into one of the leaders of the insurgent movement in Angola, build up a reputation for him among a certain section of the nationalists and make him head of the provisional government with headquarters in Leopoldville (now Kinshasa).

"Holden, in his turn, has done a lot to compromise and even murder the nationalists who for one reason or another did not suit the CIA. . . . With the help of the CIA Holden Roberto secured for his government the recognition of most of the OAU member-states. He also secured official aid from this organisation.

"It may well be said that there was a period when the Americans, acting through Holden Roberto, practically controlled the situation in Angola. And the only thing that prevented the realisation of their plans was the presence of other nationalist groups in Angola, primarily the Agustinho Neto group.

"That is why the CIA undertook various steps to get rid of Neto. Time and again Roberto's people tried to assassinate him. Simultaneously, attempts were made to subordinate Neto to Holden Roberto under the pretext of uniting the nationalist forces of Angola.

"However, all these measures did not bring the Americans the desired result. It may even be said that the effect was quite the opposite, since it helped Agustinho Neto to expose Roberto as a CIA agent and considerably reduce his influence both in Angola and all over Africa. . . ."

Since the establishment of the FNLA and GRAE, Roberto's armed detachments were practically inactive against the Portuguese colonialists, concentrating their efforts on murdering MPLA militants.

I should like to quote a document which was circulated by the MPLA in 1967 disclosing facts about the treachery of Roberto's bands.

"A horrible balance sheet.

"Instead of fighting the Portuguese Holden Roberto uses the territory of Congo (Kinshasa) to kidnap and assassinate true patriots.

"Beginning with 1961, when the liberation struggle of the people of Angola reached its peak thanks to the determination of the MPLA, Holden's group, while trying to create an impression that it was engaged in 'patriotic' activity, stepped up the kidnappings and assassinations of MPLA fighters and other Angolan patriots.

"For their operations in the interests of the Portuguese colonialists Holden and his group take advantage of the total freedom accorded to them by Congo (Kinshasa). The MPLA did not react against these fratricidal provocations so as not to pervert the struggle of our people and not to create difficulties for the fraternal people of the Congo (Kinshasa) which has given such a fraternal reception to Angolan refugees.

"But such a state of affairs can no longer be tolerated. The blood of our fallen patriots demands that this deliberate sabotage of our struggle should be immediately stopped.

"By listing the following facts we intend to show responsible Africans that the MPLA can no longer tolerate the crimes perpetrated by the so-called GRAE.

"In October 1961 in the vicinity of Fuesse Holden's bands massacred an armed MPLA group which was helping the people of Dembos region. They killed 21 patriots including Tomaz Ferreira (Commander), Daniel Castro, Manuel Guimarães, João Gomes, Rui Melo, Domingos Francisco, Sebastião Gomes, João Domingos, Jacinto Mahumba, Joaquin Francisco, Almeida Miguel, Augusto Maringo, Antonio Bastos, José Gomes, Mendes Valada, Domingos Minguel, Lueia Dungo, João Simão, Miguel and João Mateus.

"In 1962, Marcos Kassanga, UPA Chief of Staff, told a press conference that his fighters had killed more than 8,000 Angolans. The victims were chiefly MPLA members who did not know the Kikongo language and included teachers, Protestant and Catholic priests, students and mestizos all of whom wanted to fight against Portuguese colonial domination.

"Back as 1962 armed UPA bands killed their commander João Baptista Traves Pereira suspected of sympathising with the MPLA.

"On March 26, 1963, three MPLA fighters António Ambrosio, António Mubemba and Jacinto Manuel were thrown into the Louzoumu prison on the instigation of the FNLA.

"In April 1963 FNLA bands ambushed an MPLA guerrilla detachment on its way to Nambuangongo on the banks of the Loge and thirteen patriots—Gonçalo Luiz, Luis Pereira, Kabando Katoko, Domingos da Silva, Pascoal Mubau, João Gonçalves, João Mahinga, Miranda Assureira, Pedro Francisco, José Sebastião, Antonio João, Sebastião Correia and Bernardo—were killed there.

"In April 1963 Miranda Marcelino, member of MPLA Steering Committee, and Manuel Morais were kidnapped in Kifuta (Angola) and it was only thanks to their courage that they managed to escape an ignominous death.

"At about the same time four other MPLA members—Manuel João, José Cristiano, Correia and Bastos Vicente—were also kidnapped and a group of students holding MPLA scholarships who arrived from Angola to the Democratic Republic of Congo[1] were killed on the bank of the Loge just as it was about to cross it.

"António Condesse, member of the MPLA Steering Committee was arbitrarily arrested by the Congolese authorities in Kinshasa on November 22, 1963 on Holden's instigation.

"Early in 1964 another three MPLA activists, João Nekongo, Manuel Morais and Adriano Carlos were kidnapped in Kinshasa and transferred to a concentration camp in Kinkuzu. The first two are still in the camp but the third was murdered in November last after almost three years' incarceration.

"In March 1964 eight MPLA activists, including Miranda Sebastião (President of the Regional Committee of Quibaxe-Angola), José de Castro and João Augusto were kidnapped and tortured.

"In July 1964, 23 activists including responsible officials António Domingos, Conceição Bernardo (pastor) and Pascoal Vandunen (pastor) also fell into the hands of the UPA bands.

"On September 28, 1964 these bands ambushed and killed an MPLA detachment....

"Holden's agents conduct their criminal activity also in the region of Katanga. With the help of corruptive methods these agents attack Katanga authorities, abduct people and engage in systematic plunder. Fifty-five Angolan patriots fell into their hands in 1965 and 1966 and those who survived are now in Zambia....

"Only the presence of MPLA armed forces made it possible in November 1966 to free 11 activists whom the FNLA had been holding for a long period in Kinguengo...."

---

[1] Congo (Kinshasa), or Democratic Republic of the Congo, is now called Zaire.—O. I.

"In February 1966, also in Kinguengo, five MPLA activists including Joaquim Paulo (a responsible official) were abducted and since then disappeared.

"In that period several MPLA activists were kidnapped and tortured in the region of Zala. . . .

"On May 19, 1966 the same band perpetrated a horrid massacre in Kamuna (Kinshasa). The victims were 32 patriots from Nambuangongo of whom only one survived. This incident aroused the anger of the authorities of Central Kongo who were forced to intervene. A trial was held at which photos of the atrocities reminiscent of those perpetrated in Buchenwald were produced in evidence. . . .

"In August 1966, another group of MPLA activists, including José Pascoal and Fernando Miranda, was abducted in Central Congo and transferred to a camp in Kinkuzu.

"In September 1966 four MPLA activists—Simão Nelumba, Augusto Azevedo, Eduardo Kiano and Paulo Neto—were abducted in Kinshasa and at present their lives are in danger.

"Among the ten MPLA activists who were kidnapped in Kinshasa in November 1966 are commander João Gonçalves Benedito, Member of the MPLA Political Bureau and José Miguel Buta. They have been placed in the Kinkuzu camp and are threatened with death.

"In 1966, shortly before Christmas, Adriano Carlos, a responsible MPLA official, and a group of three Angolans were executed in the Kinkuzu camp.

"In January 1967 these bands of criminals left the territory of Congo (Kinshasa) and set out in pursuit of an MPLA squadron which was returning to bases in the Cuanza-Norte district. But our forces repelled the attack which was launched from ambush.

"On February 16, 1967 forty MPLA fighters on a combat assignment were intercepted by bands stationed in Kamuna, but managed to get away with great difficulty after being subjected to torture.

"On February 28 three responsible functionaries José Pascoal, Aleixo Pascoal and Salvador Francisco were dispensing assistance to Angolan refugees and the Congolese population in Songololo. They were captured. The former has disappeared while the other two have been transferred to the Kinkuzu camp.

"On March 2 twenty MPLA fighters, including five young women, responsible officials of the Organisation of the Women of Angola, ... who had been sent on an assignment, were abducted and are believed to be dead.

"On March 4, the murderer Petterson with a Congolese lieutenant kidnapped four persons in Louboumbashi and brought them to FNLA premises in a comatose state. They were Estêvão Isaac, an MPLA activist, Carlos Lengema, a student, Sullivani Jean and César Nogueira, a man from Cape Verde. ... Such raids and kidnappings are carried out regularly and it is impossible to keep track of all of them. This document lists only those cases about which we have precise information.

"By denouncing these crimes and furnishing detailed information about them, the MPLA wants to warn Africans that it is no longer possible to restrain the wrath of all the patriots of Angola. Such actions will impede the liberation struggle of our people and consequently strengthen the positions of the colonial army. Furthermore, the defensive system of the southern part of Africa will be hit.

"That is why the MPLA insists that the sagacious representatives of Africa approach the government of the Republic of Congo with a request to neutralise Holden's traitorous bands. As regards the MPLA, it will fulfil its responsibilities.

Steering Committee of the MPLA
Brazzaville, March 18, 1967."

Earlier I quoted a declaration of the Central Committee of the Democratic Party of Guinea of December 11, 1975, which said that OAU recognition of Holden Roberto's "government" dealt the liberation struggle in Angola a "terrible blow". Bearing this in mind the MPLA, developing its military successes, also took determined steps in the sphere of foreign policy in an effort to get the OAU to reverse its decision. The MPLA took into account the alignment of forces in the OAU where many African states, without going to the heart of events in Angola, demanded that the MPLA should unite with FNLA/GRAE. Although the MPLA knew that conditions for the merger did not exist it, nevertheless, strove to bring together all progressive-minded Angolans under a single banner of struggle against the colonialists. In support of the above I shall quote from a memorandum dispatched by the MPLA leadership on October 10, 1966 to the Tripartite Commission which was in session in Cairo at the time.

"Examining the question of Angola the Conference of the Heads of African States and Governments which took place in Cairo in July 1964 decided that it was necessary to take serious steps in order to achieve unity of action of the MPLA and the so-called GRAE (Revolutionary Government of Angola in Exile), although the latter was already in a state of decline.

"For this purpose and also in fulfilment of the decision passed by the First Session of this conference, a Commission of three countries was formed consisting of representatives of the United Arab Republic, Congo (Brazzaville) and Ghana. It was charged with studying methods for achieving 'concord, cooperation or unity' between different liberation movements in Angola. In other words, the Tripartite Commission was to bring about a reconciliation of the various movements, particularly the MPLA and the so-called GRAE, with the view to establishing a united political and military front.

"In response to the efforts of the Tripartite Commission, the MPLA participated in all its four meetings, while the other side was invariably absent.

"In the period from 1964 to 1966 the position of the nationalist movement in Angola changed enormously. Today it is clearer than ever before that the MPLA is unquestionably the sole combat force in Angola. And there is every reason to ask: does the so-called GRAE still exist?

"Indeed we seriously doubt that it does actually exist. What support does it get from the Angolans and what authority does it enjoy with them? What signs are there of its activity in the country?

"Neither at the Cabinda front, nor at the recently opened Moxico front, nor at any other front in the north of the country is there any evidence of the so-called GRAE. It simply does not exist.

"Therefore we should like to ask whether it is really important and necessary now to raise the question of unity between the MPLA and the so-called GRAE?

"The MPLA believes that if the esteemed Tripartite Commission makes a thorough survey it will arrive at the conclusion that the existence of the so-called GRAE should be seriously doubted.

"We would like to quote a short excerpt from a statement made by esteemed National Deputy Mr. Loran Nsinji in the

Chamber of Deputies of the Democratic Republic of Congo on September 26, 1966:

" '...Unfortunately for our Angolan brothers who enjoy our kindness and our hospitality, the so-called Angolan government in exile (GRAE) based here, in Kinshasa, violates our laws and customs by committing on our own sovereign Congolese territory acts which only a government of an independent country with a dictatorial regime can commit. Indeed, some Angolans, and they are not few, who belong to political parties which do not participate in the so-called Angolan government in exile are being persecuted in the Democratic Republic at present. These unfortunates who are with the opposition are being arrested, imprisoned and executed by the Angolans themselves. . . .'

"The MPLA has always abided by the provision inscribed in its programme of action to the effect that unity of the Angolans is a matter of prime importance for their liberation from colonial domination. Nevertheless, the MPLA has invariably encountered systematic resistance of the FNLA/GRAE in all its efforts to achieve such unity.

"It is our opinion that true unity will be attained when all fighters are united in common ranks, when it is created for the achievement of common objectives in our country.

"Even now, taking into consideration all the changes which are taking place in the history of unity, the MPLA declares that it is prepared to do everything it can to find grounds consistent with unity resting on revolutionary principles.

"Thus, in order to work out the foundation for unity with the FNLA, the MPLA proposes the following:

"a) Revision of the question of recognition of the so-called GRAE, to facilitate the achievement of unity.

"b) Immediate release of all MPLA activists held in prisons on the territory of Congo (Kinshasa) on the orders of the so-called GRAE. Termination of persecutions, arrests and exiles of Angolans, MPLA members, to the Kinkuzu base.

"c) Termination of all anti-MPLA propaganda conducted by GRAE among refugees in the Democraitc Republic of Congo.

"d) An inquiry into the activity of the FNLA and the so-called GRAE in order to ascertain whether the so-called GRAE is actually fighting for national liberation."

The Tenth Session of the OAU Council of Ministers which met in Addis-Ababa from February 20 to 24, 1968 revoked the organisation's earlier decision granting exclusive rights to Holden Roberto's government to receive assistance from the OAU, and its Committee of Liberation began to distribute assistance between the MPLA and the FNLA. In 1969 the OAU appealed to the governments of all countries to cooperate with the MPLA as the sole truly legitimate representative of fighting Angola.

The majority of the African countries abided by the OAU decision, but Roberto still received aid and support from the Kinshasa Government and military assistance and considerable sums of money continued to arrive from the United States.

Documents published in US newspapers and journals, and also the debates which took place in the US Congress would later provide concrete information about the nature and volume of assistance which Roberto and his organisation received from the CIA. But from 1969 right up to April 25, 1974 nothing was said either in Africa and elsewhere in the world about the FNLA and its "president" Holden Roberto. This organisation together with Roberto became a political corpse and when the Portuguese authorities reported that the situation was most stable in that part of Angola where there were Holden Roberto's people who displayed no activity at all, they were telling the truth.

In 1969 the Nixon Administration came to power and Washington officials reached the conclusion that it would be meaningless to dish out aid to Roberto's organisation in large portions. Here is what former adviser to Tshombe and Roberto John A. Marcum, who subsequently became dean of the California University of Santa Cruz, wrote in this connection in an article carried by *Foreign Affairs* in April 1976: "With the advent of the Nixon Administration in 1969, a major review of American policy toward southern Africa (NSSM 39)[1] concluded that African insurgent movements were ineffectual, not 'realistic or supportable' alternatives to continued colonial rule. As a result, American policy became

---

[1]NSSM 39 or National Security Study Memorandum 39 was prepared under the direction of Henry A. Kissinger when he was presidential national security adviser. This document set forth five options of future US policy in a region of Southern Africa embracing Zambia, Malawi, Rhodesia, Mozambique, Angola, South Africa, Namibia, Swaziland, Botswana and Lesotho. At the time (1970) the policy choice made by the White House was based on Option Two which contained the fol-

even more Eurocentric. The authors of the interdepartmental policy review, commissioned by the then White House adviser Henry Kissinger, questioned 'the depth and permanence of black resolve', and 'ruled out a victory at any stage'. They did not question the depth and permanence of Portuguese resolve. It was a basic miscalculation stemming from faulty intelligence in both senses of that word. By the early 1970s there were ample signs that Portugal's days as a Euroafrican power were numbered. . . ."

The MPLA was the only organisation which waged a consistent and highly successful struggle for national liberation.

In July 1970 I spent almost three weeks with an MPLA guerrilla detachment in eastern Angola and not only witnessed it in action but also witnessed how the MPLA organised the life of the civilian population in the liberated areas. I became acquainted with the results of its efforts in the fields of education and health protection and, what was very important, I saw for myself that the population fully supported MPLA policy.

Below are excerpts from my travel diary which I kept in those days.

July 8. In the morning we had our last meeting with three representatives of the MPLA leadership.

Spreading out a large-scale map of Angola on the table, Comrade Ico Carreira described the situation in the country and gave an account of the course of the struggle in different areas. The MPLA divides the country into six regions, which are subdivided into zones and the zones into sectors. We were

---

lowing premise: "The whites are here to stay [in Southern Africa—O. I.] and the only way that constructive change can come about is through them. There is no hope for the blacks to gain the political rights they seek through violence, which will only lead to chaos and increased opportunities for the communists.

"We can, by selective relaxation of our stance toward the white regimes, encourage some modification of their current racial and colonial policies and through more substantial economic assistance to the black states (a total of about $5 million annually in technical assistance to the black states) help to draw the groups together and exert some influence on both for peaceful change.

"Our tangible interests form a basis for our contacts in the region, and these can be maintained at an acceptable political cost." ("Secret Memo Bares US 'Tilt' in Africa" by Murrey Marder. *The Washington Post,* October 13, 1974.)

going to visit Zone "B" of the Third Region which bordered on Congo (Kinshasa) in the north, Namibia in the south and Zambia in the east. Zone "B" lies in the north. "We planned to show you two zones," he said, "but that will take all of three months. Comrade Neto invited you to visit any zone you want. You have chosen Zone 'B'. We shall take you there."

His words to the effect that we could visit any zone in the Third Region were fully consistent with the situation on the Angolan battlefronts. Prior to 1963 the guerrillas were mainly active in Cabinda enclave (Second Region) and also in the First and Fourth Regions adjoining Congo (Kinshasa), whereas of late the MPLA has concentrated its main forces in the Third Region which borders on Zambia. All told the MPLA is in effective control over approximately 400,000 square kilometres.

July 12. At 00.10 hours our group entered the Third Region of Angola and headed towards one of the sectors in Zone "B".

I have already said that MPLA guerrilla units are conducting active military operations in all the zones of the Third Region, and it should be noted that all the units involved maintain effective cooperation. Although they are irregulars, the guerrillas act as regular line units. Detachments based in the various zones have their specific local tasks, but all of them fulfil strategic plans drawn up by the Military-Political Coordination Committee of the MPLA headed by its Chairman Agostinho Neto.

July 18. We planned to devote the whole day to filming the life of a guerrilla detachment which has broken camp near our huts. We were in a thin jungle which differs greatly from the dense humid jungle covering dozens of kilometres closer to the equator. In a thin jungle a large area can be kept under observation and the glades look as though they have been weeded and combed. But a guerrilla detachment has to find a place where it can reliably hide itself from unfriendly eyes. The site chosen for the camp was ideal in this respect. The hastily built huts stood in glades canopied by the heavy crowns of several dozen trees. In one of the glades there were two tables made of thin poles lashed together with strips of m-samba tree bark which resembles our Russian acacia, where the men were cleaning their weapons. To the right of the huts there was a clearing where the guerrillas lined up in the mornings to receive instructions for the next 24 hours and hear the latest news from the commissar who heard it over the radio. Since not all of them understood Portuguese he repeated it in two and even three local dialects. During the line-up the men also analysed the performance of individual groups and elements back from combat assignments.

As in any other military unit the morning began with the sounding of the reveille. Rolling up their straw mats and tucking their blankets into rucksaks the men hastened to the river for a wash. Approximately 30 minutes later the commander blew a whistle summoning the men to morning exercises. After that they breakfasted and then cleaned their weapons and ammunition. Humidity was not too high in the places which we visited, but the tropics did make themselves felt and it was necessary to take every precaution to prevent rusting.

When we reached the disposition of the detachment the men had already cleaned their weapons and the commander was just about to give the final instructions to two groups (a group consisted of ten fighters) that were to replace their comrades who had been for a week on patrol duty in the direct proximity of the Portuguese garrisons.

"The assignment of Comrade Fogo's group," the commander was saying, "is to observe a sector extending from the blown-up bridge No. 3 and a wrecked Portuguese store six kilometres away from it. You will lay no ambush. You will also temporarily remove the mines which we have planted on the footpaths. In a word, we must make the enemy feel at ease and give him no cause to order combat readiness No. 1. Now all our actions, each step are geared to the fulfilment of a single task—that of successful shelling the Portuguese garrison. The enemy must not even sense our presence until the operation gets under way. . . ."

Approximately the same instructions were issued to the commander of the second group. We noticed that all the fighters left almost all their individual meat rations to the comrades remaining in the camp. It was explained to us that the sector to which they were assigned abounded in all sorts of game. The guerrillas could get fresh meat by hunting. The group took along a shotgun. Its shots would not attract the attention of the Portuguese because they did not resemble those fired from a rifle or an automatic weapon.

The groups left.

July 19. Not far from the spot where we are living there is a Revolutionary Training Centre (CIR), or simply military courses. Comrade Mono who is in charge is a short, thickset man with a massive forehead and a short beard, which he strokes with his left hand every once in a while. Mono studied in the Soviet Union for several years and has a good knowledge of Russian.

Tables and benches placed under awnings made of reed mats served as classrooms. Nearby stood a table where guns were taken apart and cleaned. Portraits of Commander Henda[1] and Chairman Neto hung from trees which surrounded the clearing. The majority of the trainees had been temporarily attached to our detachment so that only a third of their original number, about ten people, remained at the centre. The lesson which we attended was devoted to an account of the assistance received by the people of Angola from different countries.

Mono told men that the world was carefully following the struggle of the people of Angola. He explained why Portugal relied on NATO and what was NATO, where countries which were friendly towards the MPLA were situated and how the the Soviet people helped the Angolans. (Incidentally the first guerrilla groups were armed with Soviet PPSh submachine guns, and we heard many songs in Angola about them). Then the trainees spoke (there were two women among them).

July 22. This evening when we returned to the camp after filming the operations of the scouts, I had a long talk with the Commander of the Reconnaissance Group Cotondo. He became an active revolutionary ten years ago, in 1960. Believe it or not he was only 12 then. At first Cotondo served with UPA detachments. Here are a few facts from his life. When Cotondo was forced to leave his native village his brother Benguela gave him some money to pay his way to Elizabethville, where the UPA which publicised its preparations to begin a struggle for the liberation of Angola had one of its centres.

The UPA representative in the city at the time was one Jorge Alicersis Larenquin who recruited volunteers for his organisations. The UPA recruits were housed in a long,

---

[1] Commander Hogi ja Henda, a hero of the MPLA, who lost his life during an attack on a Portuguese garrison.—*O. I.*

gloomy barracks-like building on the city's outskirts. Cotondo was disenchanted with the atmosphere that reigned there. Many of the young recruits had already spent several months there, but no one trained them or let them know what their future tasks would be. There were no weapons with the exception of an old German made Mauser.

Having familiarised himself with the situation, Cotondo began to ask his comrades: "What are we here for? What do our leaders plan to do?"

The youngsters were at a loss and replied: "Jorge Larenquin said that when everything will be organised and there will be more of us, the UPA leadership will send all of us abroad for military and political training. He said that all of us will go to the United States where we'll be uniformed and trained. We'll return to Angola fully trained for the struggle."

It was all the same to Cotondo. He did not know where the United States was located, whether it was nearer or farther away than his native village. All he wanted was to begin fighting as soon as possible. But three months passed, then four, then six. The situation at the barracks remained almost the same as on the day of his arrival. True, there were some changes. For instance, food rationing grew worse and sometimes the recruits went hungry for several days at a stretch. At the same time the UPA leaders who visited the recruits, drove up in expensive cars and it was rumoured that they went to bars in the evenings spending huge sums of money which the UPA received from undisclosed sources.

Once in a while Jorge Larenquin and his aides brought leaflets to the barracks. But their text was strange. They neither described the situation in Angola nor unmasked Portugal's policy in the colonies, but urged a struggle against ... the MPLA, so that one got the impression that the main enemy of the people of Angola were not the Portuguese but the MPLA. It was even stated in the leaflets that if any UPA fighter discovers an Angolan who was an MPLA member, it was his duty to kill him.

The recruits were confined to barracks, but with time they discovered ways of sneaking out. Finally, the chief warden called a meeting of his subordinates and they decided not to prevent "UPA fighters" from earning money for food on the condition that they would spend the nights in the barracks. They took on all sorts of jobs in the city: carried crates, polished shoes, swept the streets and hung around shops help-ing people carry home their purchases. Cotondo made friends with a boy by the name of Zobe Martins and the two of them together with Cotondo's cousin Sangue do Povo who also lived in the barracks made up their minds to run away. They saved up some money, enough to pay the fare from Elizabeth-ville to Guelolo, also in the Congo, where another cousin of Cotondo lived. "There must be an organisation which wages a real struggle against the Portuguese," Cotondo would say. "I think that they are lying to us about the MPLA." And the boys ran away as they had planned.

In 1964 an MPLA guerrilla detachment entered Zone "A" of the Third Region in Angola. It included several young fighters one of whom was Cotondo who was sixteen at the time.

Ever since then he is fighting in Angola.

July 29. We have fulfilled our mission in the main and it's time for us to return. In my opinion we have photographed all that was necessary for the film. As we left we handed over a bag of medical supplies to a doctor's assistant of the local Medical Aid Service (SAM). In the Third Region SAM looks after approximately 383,000 people. I should like to point out that the MPLA has always regarded the organisation of medical assistance for the population as one of its basic tasks. The only "doctors" who were to be found in the MPLA-controlled regions prior to their liberation were the witch doctors. Seriously ill people went to them for help while others entrusted themselves to the care of old women in the villages who knew the traditional African healing crafts. Fol-lowing the opening of the eastern front the situation in Mo-xico and Cuando-Cubango regions changed. The guerrillas brought along not only the PPSh submachine guns, grenades and slogans: "Victory or death" and "Order and justice", but also opened revolutionary training centres and schools, and set up SAM stations. Now each zone of the Third Region has a medical aid station with a doctor's assistant in charge, and in each sector there is a medical nurse or an attendant. In areas where there is a shortage of medical personnel there are people who have been instructed to render first aid. In the jungle near a *kimbus* (the local word for village) there are huts with a white cloth bearing a red cross over their entrances. The first medical stations were organised in Zone "A" and the biggest of them has been named after **Amerigo**

Boavida, a guerrilla doctor who fell in action in one of the zones of the Third Region.

For the moment we cannot cite complete statistics about all the medical stations in the Third Region. Here are, however, some data concerning Zone "A" and also Zone "B" where we are at present. The Amerigo Boavida station in Zone "A" is running a course for doctors' assistants which is attended by 14 people. They are taught anatomy, pharmaceutics, administration of first aid to wounded and sick and hygiene, and gain a lot of practical experience by taking care of the wounded fighters who stop over at the station on their way to hospitals. The following figures show the increasing popularity of this station: in May 1969 it treated 111 sick; in June, 132, in August, 321, and in September of that year, 496 (these are the latest figures which are available to us).

All told Zones "A" and "B" have three doctors, 11 trained doctors' assistants, 26 medical nurses and attendants and another 14 persons who are due to complete a training course at the Amerigo Boavida station.

Of course, for the 100,000 people living in Zones "A" and "B" (the total number of inhabitants in the Third Region is 383,000) this is an infinitely small number of medical personnel. Still, it is only the beginning and judging by the above figures it is clear that the MPLA is seriously concerned with improving medical assistance in the liberated regions.

July 31. Our last day in Angola. One more effort and our group will complete its tour. And then every hour will bring nearer our homecoming to Moscow, where we shall meet our friends and go back to work at our editorial offices. Throughout our short 21-day sojourn in Angola we felt that we were with devoted friends who have the warmest feelings for our country. And that was also what the Angolan comrades said about their Soviet companions. Perhaps our internationalism and solidarity with the people of Angola are rooted precisely in the fact that we too have once lived through all that: guerrilla detachments of poorly trained, hungry and barefoot fighters, and we too passed through areas laid waste by the invaders, and through bomb-wrecked cities and villages. That is why the Soviet people who has paid a price of 20 million lives for victory in the Second World War alone cannot but take close to heart the tragedy and resolve of the people of Angola who are fighting with such dedication for independence.

There is a saying in the Soviet Union which goes back to days of the war: "I would go on a reconnaissance mission with such a comrade." Well, we spent three weeks with an MPLA guerrilla detachment. Its commanders, commissars and fighters all had different tempers and characters, but if any one of us was asked what we thought about any one of the 30 Angolan comrades we would have said: "I would go on a reconnaissance mission with him." Yes, we would have done so without a second thought. Because for us they are real men, true and sincere comrades.

Chapter III

"Judas" Savimbi Exposed

His full name is Jonas Malheiro Savimbi. But since approximately the middle of 1974 people in Angola refer to him only as "Judas". "Judas" Savimbi, chairman of the so-called National Union for the Total Independence of Angola (UNITA).

He was born in Bie in Angola into the family of a wealthy stockbreeder. He attended classes at the local American Catholic mission. In the fifties the mission gave him a scholarship which enabled him pursue his studies in Lisbon where he became a licentiate in political science and law. Possessing a practical mind Savimbi realised that the Portuguese colonial authorities would not permit him to practice law in Angola, and so he went to Switzerland. Settling down in Lausanne he got a job with an organisation calling itself the Swiss Friends of Angola. There he knocked together a group of Angolan students and called it the National Union of Students of Angola (UNEA) although there was another student organisation uniting Angolan students—the General Union of Angolan Students (UGEAN) which was a member of the International Union of Students (IUS). To counterbalance the UGEAN Jonas Savimbi promptly got his organisation into the US-controlled splitter student organisation known as the Coordinating Secretariat of the National Union of Students "International Student Conference" (COSEC/ISC). But he found little satisfaction with playing the role of an "Angolan student leader in exile". By then the MPLA had been in existence for four years already. Savimbi also knew that there was an organisation calling itself UPA in Leopoldville. And so he decided to try his luck in the political arena. In the beginning of 1960 the MPLA bureau in Conakry, the capital of the Republic of Guinea, received a letter from Lausanne written by licentiate Jonas Malheiro Savimbi. Briefly introducing himself, he mentioned his high professional training and said that he would agree to hold a leading post in the MPLA.

When the letter arrived there were several members of the MPLA leadership in Conakry. They were mildly shocked by such a proposition coming as it did from a total stranger who had never been connected with the national liberation movement of the Angolan people. Naturally, no one thought of offering a "post" of any kind to a Jonas Savimbi from Lausanne, but the MPLA needed educated people who could fulfil its assignments abroad. Some time later Savimbi received an MPLA membership form and an accompanying letter with several brochures explaining the MPLA's aims, tasks and structure and other materials, of the kind that were usually sent to progressive journals and newspapers throughout the world. The letter welcomed Savimbi's decision to take part in the work of the organisation and said that the MPLA leadership would decide how it would use him in the organisation after observing his activity for a time.

Being inordinately ambitious Savimbi began sending letter after letter to the MPLA Bureau in Conakry insisting that one of the leaders of the liberation movement should come to Lausanne. He said it was absolutely essential for him to establish direct contact with someone in the MPLA leadership because people of such calibre as himself were rare and if the organisation wanted him in its ranks it was not enough to send him a membership form.

Naturally, no member of the MPLA leadership had any intention of going to Lausanne. But, and I repeat that, since the organisation was really short of trained cadres, they sent him a ticket for a Lausanne-Conakry flight. He did not go to Conakry because as he later explained he had no guarantees that the MPLA would offer him a "leading post". In that case no one would pay his trip back to Lausanne and he would be unable to return to Switzerland. Savimbi remained in Lausanne but did not give up his plans of "making good" and decided to offer his services to the UPA. An opportunity shortly presented itself.

At the end of 1960 Holden Roberto arrived in Lausanne. Savimbi hastened to meet him and was very pleased with their conversation. Firstly, Savimbi understood that in fact Roberto had no organisation, barring its name and the group of relations who were listed among its leadership. Secondly, he was quick to see that Roberto disposed of considerable sums of money; and even if they did come from undisclosed sources, Savimbi could not have cared less. Thirdly, there was no one in Roberto's organisation with at least a minimum theoretical grounding. And, fourthly, realising that Roberto himself was a small-time operator, Savimbi convinced himself that it would be quite simple to take over his post.

In order to give himself added importance, however, Savimbi said that he would have to ponder the question of joining the UPA leadership. He even said that, if he did, he would have liked to head the UPA's International Department and thus greatly impressed Holden Roberto.

In the beginning of 1961 the COSEC/ISC invited Jonas Savimbi to take part in a student conference which it was sponsoring in Kampala. Savimbi promptly accepted the invitation mindful of the fact that the COSEC/ISC promised to take care of all travelling and hotel expenses. In Kampala he had several meetings with the prominent Kenyan politician Tom Mboya, at that time General Secretary of the Kenya African National Union (KANU). Although Mboya had already acquired a reputation of being America's man, he was undeniably a popular figure not only in Kenya but also outside her borders. Savimbi gave an account of his conversation with Roberto and Mboya urged him to join the UPA because he believed that the Americans had a very good opinion of this organisation and helped it in every way so that those who stood at its helm experienced no material difficulties.

Conversations with Tom Mboya made Savimbi make up his mind and he wrote to Roberto saying that he would join the UPA. Shortly afterward he arrived in Leopoldville and was appointed head of the International Department of UPA.

Soon Holden Roberto gave Jonas Savimbi his first assignment, sending him to New York to establish contacts with the delegations attending the Sixteenth Session of the UN General Assembly. Savimbi spent the greater part of his month-long stay in New York at the UN building on the East River and also in the bureau which the UPA opened in the city. He managed to find out a few facts about Holden Roberto's connections with the CIA, and became convinced that the Americans were set on making Roberto the leader of the national liberation movement in Angola. But their plans clashed ·with Savimbi's intention to become UPA "president".

In Cairo near the Al Tahrir Square on the bank of the Nile stands the mosaiced building of the League of Arab States. Top political leaders of the states of this region gathered on more than one occasion in League's conference hall with its giant square table to discuss their problems.

In July 1964 representatives from 33 African countries assembled at the headquarters of the League of Arab States for the Second All-African Meeting of Heads of State. The Congolese delegation flew in from Leopoldville on July 17 and as usual brought along a makeweight in the person of Holden Roberto. The GRAE "foreign minister" Jonas Malheiro Savimbi had arrived in Cairo somewhat earlier.

On July 19, the second day of the conference, all newspapers published reports on the opening ceremony, photographs of the delegates and interviews with the high guests of the Egyptian capital.

With the exception of its first and last sittings the conference worked behind closed doors so that journalists had virtually nothing to do in the building of the League of Arab States. But, as the saying goes, news flies fast, and soon it was rumoured that a member of Holden Roberto's group, namely his "foreign minister" Jonas Savimbi had circulated a letter at the conference. The letter was not mentioned in the daily press releases to the journalists and the participants in the conference declined to broach the issue. Several days later, however, it became known that Jonas Savimbi had circulated a letter announcing his resignation from the post of GRAE "foreign minister" because of the incompetency of Holden Roberto's brainchild. He presented his case as follows: "...Some African states refuse to study again the Angolan problems taking into consideration the Angolan realities.

"These realities are:

"Inefficiency of the Angolan Government in Exile.

"Thence and above all the fact that GRAE, far from increasing military action and gathering the masses, the only way to speed up Angola liberation, GRAE simply confines itself to *short-lived statements*.

"I, Jonas Savimbi, GRAE Minister of Foreign Affairs, have decided to resign of my position. . . ."

What were the actual motives behind this step? Savimbi who was not a fool realised that he could rise no higher in GRAE and that its masters would not exchange Roberto, who on top of everything had the closest links with the ruling circles of Congo (Kinshasa) which were dependent on the US, for an Angolan who did not belong to the Bakongo tribe. Consequently, he would be unable to carry through his ambitious plans in GRAE. It was dangerous for him to announce his resignation from the post of GRAE foreign minister in Kinshasa where he could be promptly assassinated as a person who was well informed about many of the dirty operations carried out by Roberto and his henchmen. He decided, therefore, to do so at the summit African conference. He felt safe in Cairo which was far away from Kinshasa. Moreover, if until then his name was almost unknown in Africa, his manoeuvre in the League of Arab States would attract universal attention and many would remember Jonas Savimbi, licentiate from Angola.

After Jonas Savimbi had quit GRAE slamming the door behind him, a number of FNLA functionaries followed suit and publicly announced their break with GRAE. Here is an open letter from GRAE representative in Vienna Fidelino Loy de Figueiredo dated July 28, 1964:

"Steering Committee
"Angolan People's Union
    'U.P.A.'
"B. P. 1205
"*Leopoldville.*
"Countryfellows,

"The resignation of GRAE Foreign Affairs Minister, Jonas Savimbi, enlightens many facts that, well examined, emphasise the tragic situation of the Angolan Revolution today.

"A shameful truth for all sincere freedom fighters. For more than three years of armed fight and despite the aid provided by the African independent states, today the fight is limited to small battles at the border. There is, therefore, a backward step. And, thus, facts come to light.

"Once their task in Angola 'almost achieved', the Portuguese are moving their soldiers to the so-called Portuguese Guinea to fight this colony's freedom fighters.

"There are some other very serious facts against FNLA (UPA-PDA) leaders' behaviour.

"Our Leopoldville leaders are wasting huge amounts. Our party chairman and GRAE leader allows himself the luxury of a last style car. Each minister has a car at his disposal while the refugees are dying of starvation. Some foreign banks have huge amounts in the name of our leaders what is a theft to our people.

"All these facts stated in Cairo were not disproved, for truth came to light. The fight is drawing back.

"As a party member and an aware freedom fighter, I cannot keep silent in face of such an evident betrayal to our people.

". . .I am completely against our leaders' behaviour and I condemn their actions. Since the present structures both of the Party and the Front do not allow any action from their militants to intervene and replace the leaders, I decide to leave my Party. Henceforth, I am no longer connected with the Angolan People's Union – UPA – neither with its youth nor student organisations. . . ."

It has been asserted that besides reading out his letter of resignation in the building of the League of Arab States, Jonas Savimbi also unmasked Roberto as a CIA agent. I have no proof that this actually took place. But later he did so in a lengthy article in the *Remarques Africaines* journal on November 25, 1964. Eleven years later, on October 24, 1975, this article was reprinted by the Lisbon newspaper *O Jornal*.

On December 12, 1964 several African newspapers published the so-called "Manifeste des Amis de l'Angola" ("Amangola"). It was signed by some twenty Angolans whose names had never been heard before, but heading the list was the name of Jonas Malheiro Savimbi. The "Manifesto" proclaimed their desire "sincerely to cooperate with the military-political organisations of Angolan patriots both inside and outside the country" on the basis of the principle that "a good Angolan never kills another Angolan".

Nothing more was heard about Amangola until the overthrow of fascism in Portugal. Jonas Savimbi also dropped out of the picture until March 13, 1966, when he announced the establishment of the National Union for the Total Independence of Angola (UNITA). In a special issue at the end of 1975 the *Tricontinental* journal said the following about this period in Savimbi's activity: "Between 1964 and 1966 he searches for a suitable buyer to whom he can offer his services and in March 1966 proclaims the establishment of the UNITA. But on what money? 'Private contributions.' Objectives? To open a guerrilla front in the centre of the eastern part of Angola to fight against 'enemy No. 1'— MPLA".

According to documents circulated by Jonas Savimbi the detachments of the UNITA and the entire leadership of this newly-baked organisation were based in Moxico region in the southeast of Angola. Savimbi opened UNITA bureaus in Egypt, in London, Brussels, Amsterdam, Stockholm, Dakar and Lusaka. UNITA representative in Belgium Jorge Valentin exemplified the type of people who spoke in behalf of this organisation on the international arena. Valentin was connected with Roberto's UPA/GRAE. Prior to 1966 he was paid by the CIA. After completing a course of study in the USA he worked for the COSEC/ISC in Leiden, the Netherlands, as "representative for Africa". In 1969, when it came to light that the COSEC/ISC was financed by the CIA, Valentin without severing his contacts with this organisation was already working for the UNITA. Prior to joining the UNITA he was regarded as one of the leading members of COSEC. He had a personal secretary and for many years was a highly influential figure in the COSEC where he conducted propaganda in favour of GRAE.

From time to time UNITA representatives published reports and bulletins claiming victories over the Portuguese colonialists. But it turned out that all these "military operations" were pure fiction. The South African journalist Al Venter working for the Bloemfontein *News/Check* journal wrote in its issue of April 12, 1968 that *only one group operated successfully in Angola, namely the MPLA* which with the help of methods similar to those used by the Mozambique FRELIMO managed to win positions in Northern and Eastern Angola. In its report (A/8023/A) covering the period ending April 1971, the UN Committee for Decolonisation gave progress report of the national liberation struggle in Angola. It stated that throughout 1969 Portuguese military bulletins noted a decreasing guerrilla activity of FNLA (GRAE) but spoke of increased MPLA activity which had begun to spread to the north and west. Beginning with 1968 not a word was said about UNITA in the Portuguese military bulletins. The UNITA, which in 1968 claimed that it had

3,000 trained fighters and extended its operations to six regions, in 1969, according to reports, confined its activity to an area southwest of Luso in the Moxico region.

Africa-watchers frequently asked themselves the question: on what funds did the UNITA exist, who supported it? True, it was known that Savimbi used to send his men for training to Peking. But the military supplies which he received at the time were so insignificant that military operations against the colonial regime were completely out of the question. In some of its issues published between 1969 and 1973 the *Afrique-Asie* journal pointed out that the UNITA was on the CIA payroll and had been set up with the view to creating a US-controlled puppet government in Angola.

While the UNITA had its bureau in Zambia, Savimbi maintained very close and permanent contacts with the US Embassy in Lusaka, particularly with James S. Cunningham. A CIA agent, Cunningham was in charge of political matters at the Embassy and was connected with functionaries from the American organisation National Association for the Advancement of Coloured People (NAACP) whose Executive Secretary for many years was Roy Wilkins. On page 124 in Juliuss Mader's *Who's Who in CIA* we find the following information about James S. Cunningham: "Cunningham, Dr. James S. Born 25.4 1911; speaks Spanish; 1942/46 US Army Lieutenant; since 1951 in the employ of the State Department, and works for the CIA. Was stationed in Mexico, Tegucigalpa, Asuncion, Montevideo (First Secretary), Washington." Such was the service record of the man from the CIA who guided Jonas Savimbi in Lusaka.

In 1967 UNITA was expelled from Zambia, but as the French newspaper *Le Monde Diplomatique* wrote on September 18, 1970, beginning with 1968 Savimbi frequently visited Zambia and lived in Livingstone under the guise of a fisherman.

The OAU neither recognised nor assisted Jonas Savimbi's organisation. Articles were published in some African newspapers intimating that Jonas Savimbi and the UNITA were financed by the South African racialists. But there were no documents corroborating this, just as there was no documentary proof of UNITA's links with the CIA.

The truth became known after the fall of the fascist regime in Portugal, when a large number of classified documents of the Lisbon regime were brought to the knowledge of the public. In July 1974, the *Afrique-Asie* journal published four letters that shed light on Savimbi's UNITA and proved that he was in the service of the Portuguese secret police, PIDE, and the Portuguese Military Intelligence. Below is a portion of Jonas Savimbi's correspondence with the Command of the Portuguese military units in Angola.

First letter (abridged version). From Jonas Savimbi to General Luz Cunha.

"...The difficulties of the clandestine struggle, the realities of life in Angola and perspectives for an equitable solution of the problems facing the population of this territory enable me to foresee the course of developments in Angola. Whatever the distance which will have to be covered before a final solution is found, we are confident that the authorities are already close to victory thanks to the enormous funds which are at their disposal ... thanks to the Government's policy of renovation in continuity. As far as we are concerned, we ardently desire to bring about an end of the war in the eastern sector. We have done everything possible to weaken the common enemy. ...

"On the basis of our analysis we can conclude that the MPLA is the main obstacle to peace not only in the east, but throughout Angola. The firsthand information at our disposal gives us grounds to believe that the MPLA is preparing fresh ambushes and operations against the armed forces, against the UNITA and intends to dislodge the UPA from Zaire by uniting with the UPA.

"Zaire knows that once it has dislodged the UPA from zones bordering on Angola, the MPLA will without delay launch subversive actions against the Kinshasa regime itself. General Mobutu's cautiousness rests on two factors only:

"a) The position which the Americans might adopt in connection with the manoeuvre of the MPLA–UPA merger. But history proves fairly convincingly that American policy is very inconstant and always late, they act only when their interests are concerned. The Great Powers are flirting with the OAU and no one can be sure that the United States will not for the umpteenth time erroneously assess the problems of Africa.

"b) The political errors which through ambition General Mobutu can commit in Zaire and which will arouse discontent in his army. . . . Such errors are always fatal for the frail regimes in our independent Africa.

". . .UNITA continues to maintain cells of activists in Zambia in spite of the Zambian Government's hostility towards us. It does not even display ordinary tolerance. But we have the support of the population which informs us of MPLA activity in Zambia, about its hostile intentions towards us inside the country, and even about the plans of the Government of Kaunda, who in 1970 participated together with the MPLA in elaborating measures aimed at liquidating the UNITA in Angola. But because these plans fell through Kaunda prohibited all UNITA representatives to live in Zambia or to pass through her. . . . Nevertheless, we are trying to reinforce the work of our activists in Zambia for it would be imprudent to wage a defensive war without information about the MPLA.

". . .Our stand is irreversible. We are no longer interested either in the OAU, or in modern Zambia and least of all in an alliance with the MPLA. Though certain aspects of UNITA's policy are still insufficiently clear to the Angolan authorities and the nation, one fact is irrefutable: we are actively participating in weakening the MPLA in some regions of the east (this is confirmed by the MPLA which, following the opening of the Eastern Front, accuses the UNITA of allying with the Portuguese in the struggle against it). We should harbour no illusions about entering into any alliance with people who had fought against us and are indefatigably fighting against us at present. Whatever the intentions of the government . . . we entertain no illusions about once again taking up arms against the authorities. We shall use them to force the MPLA eventually to withdraw from the Eastern regions . . .

"Furthermore, to achieve peace in the East it is necessary to:

"a) weaken the MPLA forces in Angola right up to their complete liquidation. This can be achieved by the combined efforts of the military and militarised forces and the forces of the UNITA;

"b) to liquidate MPLA camps in those regions of Zambia which border on Angola. This can be best accomplished by the UNITA because we have no political status that would warrant a political complaint to international bodies. . . . Our plans have already passed the initial stage. . . .

"c) discredit the MPLA.... By doing so we intend to strike a blow at the OAU at least as far as the liberation movements are concerned. Once the MPLA is weakened or liquidated in the East, wide prospects will open before us....

"...We have discovered the following MPLA bases:

"1) Mushukula with 20 guerrillas armed with carbines and submachine guns; Lioko with 15 people armed with submachine guns and a light machine gun; Muanamunguela with 10 men equipped with carbines, machine guns and mine-throwers. Sometimes there were more than 30 men in this camp. This was when they planned operations against UNITA or reinforced their zones in Quembo....

"2) There are other camps: Nguvu with 20 guerrillas ... and a field hospital with Dr. Eduardo dos Santos in charge; Litapi with 10 or 15 men ... their mission is to maintain liaison with Cassamba, Chavuma and Balovale.

"There are several camps on the line from Kalabo to Cuando-Cubango, the largest of which is Shikongo which has at least fifty men equipped with weapons which are usually at the disposal of the MPLA, a military instructor, a doctor, several medical attendants, a political commissar and three instructors. They are trying to build a school there with Denmark's aid....

"...I would like to add to this memorandum, which I endeavoured to make as frank as possible, a request of particular importance to me. I repeat my request to Your Excellency to supply us with at least 1,500 rounds of 7.62-calibre ammunition since in our operations against the MPLA and UPA we use weapons of this calibre....

Lungué-Bungo, September 26, 1972"

Second letter. From Jonas Savimbi to Chief of Staff of the Eastern Military Zone.

"Esteemed Senhor Armenio Nuno Ramires de Oliveira,
Lieutenant-Colonel of the Expeditionary Corps,
Chief of Staff of the Eastern Military Zone,
Luso

"...Several days ago I asked our Captain Clemente to thank you for sending 7.62-calibre rounds, and also to express our satisfaction with the fact that each meeting of ours brings us closer to the aims which we intend to achieve in conjunction with each other.

"We have already conducted an operation against the UPA men on October 12 of this year. As soon as we discovered the base which was indicated in the two messages which you have so kindly sent to me, we ascertained that it had been abandoned by UPA men. Without losing time our group of fighters set out in pursuit. The encounter took place in the vicinity of Sulá near the Imonomono which flows into the Cassai.

"This was in Zone I.

"On October 13 of this year, our forces conducted an operation against the MPLA. An MPLA group numbering 20 people 17 of whom were armed penetrated the region, carried out an operation and then headed for Quembo, a circumstance which prevented us from warning the command of your Eastern Zone. Our men pursued the group as far as Cassingo.

"...We have information that there are three more enemy bases in the given area near the rivers Carilongue and Luela and, lastly, in Chissimba. Each base has not more than 20 guerrillas. In this connection we request Your Excellency to approach the General commanding the Eastern Zone to grant us permission to operate in zones 2 and 3 beginning with November 5 for a month's period and only until our planned operation is completed. After that we shall promptly withdraw our forces from these zones.

"Several days ago we seized a 7.92-calibre MG machine gun from the UPA men.

"I was wondering whether we could send this machine gun to you for repairs, for we can put it to good use.

"Availing myself of the opportunity I should like to remind you that through Captain Clemente I asked you urgently to return to us one Baptista Sassala who tried to establish UPA cells in our UNITA. . . .

"I have just received a UPA document which I hold to be of exceptional importance. It contains detailed information about arms deliveries to the MPLA and other movements operating in Portuguese territories: the quantity and types of weapons, their cost, means of supply and so forth. . . . I regard this document as useful because it reflects the spirit which reigned at the latest conference of the heads of African states who met in Rabat in June this year.

"As soon as I have studied this document I shall send it to you through the usual channels because it would be a pity if it should be lost.

"As regards the possibility of our meeting, I am always ready to meet you and your people. . . .

Jonas Malheiro Savimbi,
UNITA President, Villa Luso,
October 25, 1972"

Third letter. From Lieutenant-Colonel Ramires de Oliveira to Jonas Savimbi.

"November 4, 1972. . .
"Eastern Military Zone.
Order No. A-5297/2

". . . I have been instructed by His Excellency the Commander of the Eastern Military Zone to inform you of our decisions on the points contained in your memorandum of September 26, 1972 and also to reply to your letter of October 25 which was received on October 31, 1972.

"1) Your analysis of the subversive movements in Angola, both inside the country and on the international scene, as well as their relations between themselves and with the African countries, has been duly studied and highly assessed. As I have already had occasion to inform you it coincides in the main with our own analysis.

"2) We agree with you that the cells of activists which the UNITA continues to maintain in Zambia may be effectively used for the following purposes: gathering information about the activity of the MPLA and the political situation in Zambia and other African states; maintaining pressure on the Zambian Government to make it change its policy towards Portugal. . . .

". . . 6) We regard the destruction of MPLA bases abroad a matter of extreme importance.

"But we also believe that this should be done only if there are definite guarantees for success and with every precaution so as not to compromise the national authorities.

"7) Your forces may operate in zones 2 and 3 until the end of November. But they must not transcend the limits of these zones because military operations are being planned in the south, particularly in the direction of the Luela and Carilonque rivers. Availing myself of the opportunity I should like to congratulate you on the results attained in the struggle against the common enemy.

"8) As regards the assistance which should be given to the population, medical supplies, seeds for sowing, cattle, books and school things have already been sent. . . .

"10) It would be very useful if you would temporarily let us have the OAU document which you have mentioned. . . . We shall make a photocopy of it and immediately return it to you.

"11) We agree to examine with your delegation the specific details of our conference with you.

"As usual you will name the date for the meeting. The main points on the agenda could be:

"a) UNITA action against the MPLA and UPA on national territory;

"b) the activity of UNITA cells in Zambia;

"c) utilisation of the Luanguinga corridor by the UNITA;

"d) attacks by UNITA detachments on MPLA bases abroad;

"e) installation of a receiving and transmitting radio station;

"f) necessary aid to the population of Lungué-Bungo;

"g) procedure for exchanging information. . . ."

Fourth letter. From Jonas Savimbi to Lieutenant-Colonel Ramires de Oliveira.

"November 7, 1972

". . . Occupation in the sector which has been assigned to us will largely depend on greater tolerance on the part of the authorities for the movement of our forces in Zone 1. In view of the situation this problem should be discussed with maximum lucidity. It is all the more important to do so because thanks to its flirtation with the MPLA the UPA has already received, according to very reliable sources, a quantity of weapons from the OAU. Nevertheless, I intend to follow your instructions although I shall invariably uphold my point of view. My strategy is better adapted to the movement of small detachments than to large forces which are at the disposal of Your Excellency.

"Since my arrival in Angola we have cultivated many fields in all regions where the UNITA is stationed thus enabling us to satisfy our requirements in food without becoming a burden for the people. . . .

"But when we deploy our detachments in deserted regions we find it difficult to keep them there and this breeds indiscipline.

"The map of the regions assigned to the UNITA was compiled with consideration for the global strategy of the struggle in the eastern part of Angola against the subversive movements, rather than for the contribution which the UNITA might make to struggle against the MPLA and UPA. I have accepted the situation and ask for nothing more, but I know that our role is restricted to our current actions. For instance, the region assigned to us in the Luando Zone is much too small, and when our detachments were withdrawing from Sachingimbu to Kamono near the Chichi river, they found themselves outside of it.

"As a result a few days ago a group of military who arrived from Munhango attacked the village of Satanda where they killed a woman and captured another. I did not report this to the authorities in the hope that one day they will appreciate our good will and the desire to fight against this war, which no longer benefits any side. It is necessary definitively to resolve all differences in the spirit which was expressed by His Excellency Professor Marcelo Caetano. But an equitable solution of the problems of the eastern part of Angola can no longer come either from Lisbon nor even from Luanda; although from the strategic and political points of view it should come from the top, from the tactical point of view, practical solutions of local problems should be found at a lower level. . . .

> . . . *Jonas Malheiro Savimbi*"

These four letters irrefutably prove the actual role played by the UNITA and Jonas Savimbi. They show that at least from the beginning of 1972 Jonas Savimbi was an agent of the Portuguese colonialists. Immediately following their publication in *Afrique-Asie* he tried to deny their existence and refute the facts they presented.

During my last visit to Angola in October 1975 I saw in *Diario de Luanda* fresh documents confirming the treacherous role which was played by Jonas Savimbi and his band. Here is the text of two of them.

Fifth letter (document).

"Copy No. ....

"Luanda, May 23, 1973

"Joint Directive 'Madeira'

"From Governor-General of Angola and Commander-in-Chief of the Armed Forces of Angola

"To the Commander of the Eastern Military Zone.

"Concerning: a. Directive of His Excellency Minister for Overseas Territories to the Governor-General Concerning UNITA.

"b. Information No. 69RO of March 28, 1973 for SGDN.

"c. Letter from the Chief of the Office of the Governor-General to Dr. Savimbi.

"1. The purpose of this directive is to define the main principles forming the basis for the development of contacts with the UNITA (operation 'Madeira') which should be carried into effect in view of the need to:

"a) ensure collaboration with UNITA armed forces in the struggle against the enemy both in the national territory and abroad;

"b) achieve the reintegration of the UNITA and the population under its control into the framework of the national community.

"2. The Commander of the Eastern Military Zone represents the Governor-General of Angola and the Commander of the Armed Forces in Angola in all matters concerning collaboration with and reintegration of the UNITA.

"For this purpose the necessary contacts will be continued between Dr. Savimbi, Chief of UNITA, or his representatives with the Command of the Eastern Military Zone (working group 'Madeira' mentioned above).

"3. Henceforth the Command of the Eastern Military Zone must:

"a) reaffirm the earlier guarantees concerning re-integration:

"–deliver the letter mentioned in paragraph 'c' to Dr. Savimbi;

"—enter into necessary correspondence with him thus strengthening contacts;

"—renew the passes at the disposal of Dr. Savimbi.

"b) continue to act in keeping with the formulated course in order to create conditions for closer contacts with the representatives of the UNITA or directly with its leader.

"4. In the sphere of cooperation:

"a) the zone where the UNITA is deployed at present will not be enlarged. It may be assigned sectors for operations against the enemy, but they will always be of a temporary nature and controlled and coordinated by the Command of the Eastern Zone;

"b) request Dr. Savimbi to indicate the socio-economic and information spheres inside and outside the country in which he intends to act without affecting the existing situation and secrecy;

"c) draw up an estimate of expenditures for the current year to cover economic, social and other forms of assistance which we cannot extend to the UNITA pending the elaboration of a definitive form in which this assistance will be furnished with the view to reintegration.

"5. As regards reintegration:

"a) the reintegration of the UNITA will pass through the following successive phases: in the first phase the UNITA must remain a clandestine organisation so that it will be able to collaborate in the struggle against the enemy on national territory or provoke acts abroad thus enabling it to operate on the international scene;

"b) to ascertain Dr. Savimbi's opinion how the reintegration plan should be formulated in order to preserve UNITA's current state as a clandestine organisation both inside the country and abroad, at least throughout the first phase;

c) in due time more detailed instructions concerning the reintegration of the UNITA will be communicated to the Command of the Eastern Military Zone. In the meanwhile we request the Command to name those people who in its view could take part in carrying through the reintegration plan.

"6. The Commander of the Eastern Military Zone may propose to include other people whom he may deem necessary in the working group 'Madeira', but bear in mind that their number should be as small as possible out of security considerations.

"Governor-General Fernando Santos e Castro
"Commander-in-Chief General Joaquim da Luz Cunha
"Distribution:
"Copy No. 1—general in command of Eastern Military Zone.
"Copy No. 2—Chief Secretariat for National Defence.
"Copy No. 3—Governor General of Angola.
"Copy No. 4—QG-CCFAA.
"Copy No. 5—QG-CCFAA."

Finally, the sixth letter. From the Chief of the Office of the Governor-General of Angola to Dr. Jonas Savimbi.
"Esteemed Senhor Dr. Jonas Malheiro Savimbi,
"His Excellency the Governor-General has entrusted me to convey best wishes to Your Excellency and inform you that he attaches importance to questions you have raised in your letters of January 11 and February 23, 1973.
"Evidently, Senhor Doctor has already had the opportunity to learn that during his visit to the Bié region, His Excellency made a number of profoundly significant remarks concerning your person and your associates. In this connection His Excellency has entrusted me to apprise you of the following:
"1. In line with the principles it invariably upholds, the Government has received with great satisfaction your proposals for reconciliation and reintegration into the national community.
"The undertaking never to resort to arms against the national armed forces which you have expressed in your letter of January 11 of the current year is yet another fact which has created a very favourable impression and we trust the sincerity of your intentions because UNITA scrupulously fulfils its commitments.
"As regards the national and local government Senhor Doctor may rest assured that we shall fulfil our guarantees set forth in the letter of March 1, 1972 and solemnly promise that no official body will demand an account from you or your associates for the actions which you conduct inside or outside the national territory.

"We do not doubt that Senhor Savimbi will not jeopardise the commitments assumed by the Portuguese State in Angola. I should like to remind you that the Chairman of the Council of Ministers Professor Marcelo Caetano repeatedly affirmed our preparedness to enter into any negotiations concerning the return and integration within the framework of the Portuguese homeland of all those who had abandoned it.

"2. In keeping with the joint decision of the Governor-General and the Commander-in-Chief of the Armed Forces in Angola the Command of the Eastern Zone will continue to represent the government at the negotiations on reintegration which we should like to conduct as quickly as possible after the specific positions bearing upon common interests have been defined.

"To facilitate this mission we should be most grateful if you would transmit your considerations on this matter to the Command. . . .

Chief of the Office
João Nolasco Totta"

In the next chapter I shall quote another document proving that Savimbi maintained very close ties with the Portuguese colonialists right up to the downfall of fascism.

When in July 1974 the *Afrique-Asie* published the documents which exposed the traitorous role played by Jonas Savimbi and his organisation, the UNITA "president" fiercely and indignantly refuted the authenticity of the letters. But even prior to the appearance of the journal's July issue it became known that for many years Jonas Savimbi had the closest contacts with the command of the colonial army in Angola.

I have before me the June 6, 1974 issue of the newspaper *A Provincia de Angola* with an article by Carlos Mendes, its correspondent in Luso, dated June 4. "Almost eight days have already passed since hostilities have been practically terminated in the centre of eastern Angola, or to be precise in the western part of the Moxico province where the UNITA was deployed and carried out its operations in recent years, *and where at the same time contacts were established*

CIA agent, traitor to the Angolan people Holden Roberto

Padre António de Araújo Oliveira who liaised between the
Command of the Portuguese colonial troops and Jonas Savimbi

FNLA camp in Carmona, in
Northern Angola

A torture chamber set up by
the FNLA in Luanda when the
provisional government was in
power in the Angolan capital

Refugees seeking safety in Luanda from the savageries of South African troops

Luso, 15 de Fevereiro de 1974

Ex.mo Senhor

Secretário-Geral do Estado de Angola

L U A N D A

Ex.mo Sr. Secretário-Geral

Respeitosos cumprimentos.

Lamento vir roubar um pouco de tempo a quem precisa dele
todo para o serviço da causa pública. Acontece que nas actuais circunstâncias
e após o encontro último com os representantes da UNITA (14/2/1974), julguei
de toda a conveniência dirigir-me a V. Ex. com a única finalidade de expor algumas impressões pessoais e arriscar sugestões.

Tudo isto deveria ser feito pessoalmente porque muitas vezes
a expressão escrita trai o pensamento ou, pelo menos, coarcta o alcance que se
quer imprimir à ideia. Vou tentar ser claro para que se não gerem os mal-enten-
didos que emperraram a marcha das negociações no passado.

1) Marcou-se novo encontro para o dia 28 deste. O Dr. Savim-
bi deve comparecer em pessoa "para andarmos mais depressa".(Cf. carta Savimbi de
10/2/1974). Esperará alguma proposta da nossa parte; nós aguardamos isso mesmo
do outro lado... Eis a razão porque desejo receber instruções sobre a maneira
como me conduzir nesse dia.

2) Uma questão agora relacionada com o cessar-fogo. Interes-
sa-nos realmente? Quais as condições, modalidades e finalidades do mesmo? Apenas
gerador de ambiente propício a conversações sérias?

Compreendo que se vá protelando pelo nosso lado a aborda-
gem desse problema à espera dos resultados da campanha militar em curso. Mas na-
da impede que se vá falando no assunto até porque as conversações são a espaços
de 15 dias, dando tempo a que se vá agindo conforme os resultados das operações
em curso.

3) Os meus esforços pessoais, bem evidentes na minha c a
Dr. Savimbi de 13/2/1974, vão todos no sentido de operar o degelo e ao

Photocopy of a letter to the Portuguese colonial authorities from
Padre Oliveira in which he reports on his talks with Savimbi

po convencê-los da nossa boa vontade para o fim pacífico do conflito.

4) Tenho ido mais além. Falei da utilidade dum encontro de V. Ex.cia com o Dr. Savimbi. A meu ver, é esta a única via de se chegar a um entendimento. Estarei a transmitir realmente a vontade de V. Ex.cia neste momento?

Pormenores como local, data, segurança seriam questões a abordar posteriormente.

5) Uso todas as minhas influências para que a UNITA reduza ao mínimo a crueldade desta guerra. Têm sido cavalheiros, pelo menos até ao presente, no cumprimento das promessas que me foram feitas, embora se queixem de que por parte dos Flechas não haja igual procedimento.

Durante todo o dia 10 passado estiveram emboscados na estrada Luso- -Henrique de Carvalho. Passaram muitos civis mas apenas fizeram fogo sobre forças paramilitares que apareceram ao cair da noite; têm poupado pessoal e carros dos madeireiros; evitam incomodar os muitos civis que, como eu, circulam na picada Luso- -Chicala... Devemos pensar numa que correspondência a este sinal de humanidade que, longe de nos diminuir, vai aumentar a confiança no nosso lado.

6) Ouso fazer uma proposta. Não seria possível para já e enquanto houver contactos, interditar a zona das conversações a forças militares? Apenas uma faixa compreendida entre o Lungué-Bungo e a linha do CFB, indo da Chicala até Cachipoque. Viriam ao encontro das insinuações do Dr. Savimbi e englobaria a zona onde se encontra o Sr. Cornélio Antunes(Sabino), principal negociador da UNITA até este momento.

Peço desculpa por esta liberdade e franqueza de opiniões e sugestões. Foram apenas ditadas por um desejo bem cristão de congraçar irmãos desavindos, e pelo sentimento plenamente português de querer contribuir para a pacificação da nossa terra.

Apesar da largueza desta, fico insatisfeito, esperando de futuro expor pessoalmente tudo a V. Ex.cia. As deslocações a Luanda podem ser feitas pela TAAG por serem mais discretas e menos onerosas para a Fazenda.

Sempre à disposição de V. Ex.cia

Atenciosamente,

P. António de Araújo Oliveira

Relatório sobre o acordo Mobutu - Spínola

No sábado, 14 de Setembro de 1974, o presidente Spínola e o presidente Mobutu encontraram-se e conversaram durante cinco horas na ilha do Sal, uma das ilhas do arquipélago de Cabo Verde.

As conversações versaram sobre o destino que os dois chefes de Estado entendem reservar a Angola, ao seu povo e aos seus recursos naturais. O encontro teve lugar a convite especial de Spínola. Cada parte aí apresentou as suas exigências e definiu a sua posição.

O general Mobutu solicitou de Spínola, em primeiro lugar o apoio a Holden Roberto em Angola, amputada da sua província de Cabinda, em segundo lugar que confiasse, por um lado, Angola a uma equipa dependente conjuntamente de Spínola e Mobutu, por outro lado, Cabinda, cujo subsolo contém imensos jazigos de petróleo a uma segunda equipa saída de uma certa «Frente de Libertação do Enclave de Cabinda», instalada em Kinshasa; esta segunda equipa dependeria igualmente de Spínola e Mobutu. Em terceiro lugar, Spínola deveria ajudar Mobutu à realização daquilo que este último chamou uma Federação Zaire-Angola-Cabinda tendo Mobutu como Presidente e, eventualmente, Holden Roberto como vice-presidente.

Estes são os três pontos apresentados por Mobutu a Spínola durante o encontro. Spínola aceitou estas propostas com três condições.

Em primeiro lugar, Mobutu deveria ajudar a equipa de Spínola junto de certos chefes de Estado africanos com o fim de desembaraçar diplomaticamente o Governo português no plano internacional e permitir-lhe adquirir uma certa honorabilidade, à sombra da qual ele poderia empreender com eficiência, uma nova política colonial, e no interior de Portugal, uma política de restauração da ordem.

Mobutu aceitou esta exigência. Em segundo lugar, Spínola exigiu de Mobutu que todas as sociedades capitalistas, portuguesas e multinacionais, actuassem sob a cobertura de Portugal, dispondo livremente, e durante o mínimo de vinte anos, dos imensos recursos naturais de Angola, Cabinda e Zaire. Esta exigência foi igualmente aceite por Mobutu.

Em terceiro lugar, Spínola pediu a Mobutu que o ajudasse a recuperar Moçambique e a Guiné-Bissau, não só provocando golpes de Estado, como procedendo a assassinatos por meio de infiltrações de mercenários e da corrupção de certos quadros dos Movimentos de Libertação. Neste caso igualmente Mobutu aceitou as exigências.

Photocopy of an article on the Spínola-Mobutu talks carried by an Angolan newspaper

b. Solicitar ao Dr. Savimbi opinião e sugestões quanto ao modo como o processamento da reintegração deve ser planeado, tendo em atenção os requisitos de clandestinidade, tanto no interior como no exterior, pelo menos na 1ª. fase.

c. Oportunamente serão enviadas ao Cmd da ZML instruções mais por menorizadas, relativas ao processamento da Reintegração da UNITA. Solicita-se, no entanto, desde já, o envio de elementos que esse Comando considere que devam ser incluídos no Plano de Reintegração.

6. O Comandante da Zona Militar Leste poderá propor a inclusão no Grupo DE TRABALHO MADEIRA de outros elementos julgados necessários, convindo porém restringi-lo ao menor número possível, por razões de segurança.

O GOVERNADOR-GERAL   O COMANDANTE-CHEFE

FERNANDO SANTOS E CASTRO   JOAQUIM DA LUZ CUNHA
                                                        GENERAL

DISTRIBUIÇÃO:

Exemplar nº 1 - General Comandante da ZML

Exemplar nº 2 - Secretariado Geral da Defesa Nacional

Exemplar nº 3 - Governo Geral de ANGOLA

Exemplar nº 4 - QG/CCFAA

Exemplar nº 5 - QG/CCFAA

MUITO SECRETO

Photocopy of a secret document
on talks between the Portuguese
and Savimbi

Gabinete do Governador-Geral

EXCELENTÍSSIMO SENHOR

DR. JONAS MALHEIRO SAVIMBI

Sua Excelência o Governador Geral encarrega-me de apresentar a V. Exª. os melho-
res cumprimentos e testemunhar-lhe o apreço e a importância que lhe têm merecido
os assuntos tratados nas suas cartas de 11JAN73 e de 23FEV73.

Aliás, o Sr. Dr. já teve oportunidade de verificar que Sua Excelência, visitando
o distrito do Bié, fêz algumas considerações, de profundo significado, que envol-
vem a sua pessoa e a dos seus colaboradores.

E, portanto, neste contexto que Sua Excelência me encarrega de lhe representar o
seguinte:

1. No respeito aos princípios que sempre tem afirmado, o Governo acolheu com vi-
   va satisfação os seus votos de reconciliação e de reintegração na comunidade
   nacional.

   E o compromisso de nunca mais pegar em armas contra as Forças Nacionais que
   reiterou na carta de 11JAN do corrente ano é outro facto que muito se apre-
   ciou e em que sinceramente se acredita porque a UNITA o tem respeitado com
   exemplar escrúpulo.

   Da parte do Governo Nacional e Estadual tem o Sr. Dr. as garantias constantes
   do despacho de 0IMAR72 e o compromisso solene de que em nenhuma instância vos
   serão pedidas contas, a si ou às pessoas que lhe estão afectas, das activida-
   des que, porventura, hajam levado a efeito dentro ou fora do território nacio
   nal.

   Sem embargo de reconhecer que o Sr. Dr. não põe em causa o valor dos compro-
   missos tomados neste Estado Português de Angola, gostaria de lhe recordar que
   o Presidente do Conselho de Ministros, Prof. Marcelo Caetano, tem afirmado,
   repetidamente, que estamos prontos para todas as conversas que tenham por
   objecto o regresso à sua terra e à integração na Pátria Portuguesa daqueles
   que nos abandonaram.

2. O Comando da Zona Militar Leste, por determinação conjunta do Governador-Geral
   e do Comandante-Chefe das Forças Armadas de Angola, continuará a representar o
   Governo na fase em curso do processo de reintegração que se deseja acelerar
   com vista ao reajustamento de posições e definição das questões que interessem
   à concretização do objectivo comum.

MUITO SECRETO

MUITO SECRETO

REPÚBLICA PORTUGUESA
PROVÍNCIA DE ANGOLA

Gabinete do Governador-Geral

Para o efeito de facilitar a missão, muito grato ficaria se o nosso ilustre interlocutor apresentasse àquele Comando todas as sugestões que lhe ocorrerem sobre o caso.

Entretanto, pode V. Exª. ficar ciente de que:

a) A reintegração na Comunidade Nacional abrangerá também todos os filiados da UNITA residentes no estrangeiro, dirigentes ou activistas, que o Dr. Savimbi indicar;

b) A todos os seus membros é reconhecido o direito, na conformidade da lei vigente, ao desempenho de funções públicas para que tenham preparação adequada;

c) Será muito apreciada a contribuição activa que continue a dar-nos, findo o processo de reintegração, para a Paz em Angola;

Pelo exposto, aguarda Sua Excelência que se prograda com firmeza no caminho que vem sendo seguido, por forma a que os Objectivos comuns sejam atingidos com a necessária brevidade, animados da fé que nos é legítimo possuir com base nos resultados já obtidos.

A BEM DA NAÇÃO

Repartição de Gabinete do Governo-Geral de Angola, em Luanda, aos 23 de Maio de 1973

O CHEFE DO GABINETE

JOÃO NOLASCO TOTTA

MUITO SECRETO

Photocopy of a letter from the Chief of the Office of the Governor-General of Angola to Dr. Jonas Savimbi

Fleeing from UNITA bands

A refugee

A mercenary

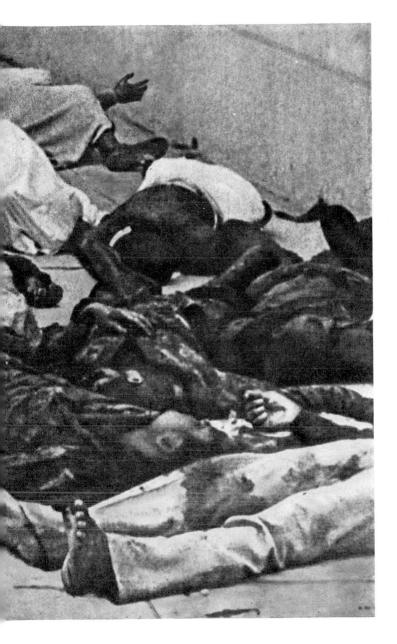

Angolan civilians massacred by
FNLA

British mercenaries departing for Angola to fight for the FNLA and UNITA

This is a mercenaries-needed ad in the US-published *Soldiers of Fortune*

with the view to leading them up to negotiations, contacts which were not always well accepted by the military authorities at the time. (Emphasis added–O.I.)

"Four years ago these contacts became more frequent. This was in line with the desire of the UNITA leader Jonas Savimbi, who beginning with the first day of his revolt against colonialism decided against putting forward extremist demands typical of other liberation movements. . . .

"Jonas Savimbi ... as we have already said was in Angola during the past several years together with his men and inhabitants of the region who went with him into the jungle. He intensified the struggle and at the same time strengthened contacts with civilians and military. These contacts could have been very fruitful if he succeeded in overcoming the inflexibility of the military who feared that such contacts could be viewed as treachery. Many senior officers who were well informed about the position of the UNITA by its leader, tried to pave the way for mutual understanding. But this proved impossible in view of the opposition of top commanders who have since been justly sacked."

Thus, this article confirmed the documents whose existence became known only a month and a half later and which irrefutably proved the treacherous role played by Jonas Savimbi, agent of the colonial troops in Angola.

We have traced the activity of two traitors of the Angolan people, Holden Roberto and Jonas Savimbi, right up to the downfall of Portuguese fascism. On April 25, 1974 Movement of the Armed Forces with the support of the people put an end to the hateful regime. One of the basic tasks which confronted new Portugal was to stop the colonial war and carry through decolonisation with the least delay. The patriots of Guinea (Bissau), Mozambique and Angola acquired ample opportunities for bringing their long and heroic struggle for independence to a victorious conclusion.

How did the initial period of the decolonisation process in Angola pass?

The world public opinion was aware that the MPLA headed by its chairman Agostinho Neto was the only force which fought against the colonial regime in Angola. It would have been natural to expect that the new Portuguese regime would begin negotiations on transferring power precisely to this national liberation organisation, and the majority of people in Portugal was of this opinion. But in view of the domination of imperialist monopolies in Angola and the stand of the then President of Portugal General António de Spínola who would not even consider entering into negotiations with the MPLA on the question of transferring power in Angola into its hands, the Angolan people had to cover a thorny path before they managed to achieve their cherished goal.

Chapter IV

Neocolonialists Hatch
a Conspiracy

One, very important circumstance played into the hands of the enemies of Angolan independence. In 1973 the then Vice-Chairman of the MPLA Daniel Chipenda caused a split in the organisation by his tribalistic, adventuristic manoeuvres. As a result when the fascist regime in Portugal was overthrown on April 25, 1974, the MPLA lacked much of its former strength. Backed by influential circles in Zambia Chipenda tried to seize power in the organisation and thus render a service to those elements in Portugal, including General Spínola, who were opposed to negotiating independence with the MPLA. It would have also greatly benefited certain groups in Angola which dreamt of establishing white minority rule in the country and in this way turn her into a second Rhodesia, and also the regime of Mobutu who had his mind set on gaining possession of the Angolan enclave of Cabinda and the northern provinces of Angola.

And so the conspiracy against Angola and the MPLA began to ripen. In order to carry it through it was not enough for the conspirators to be assured of the services of Daniel Chipenda, and so they decided to push two other traitors of the Angolan people, Holden Roberto with his FNLA and Jonas Savimbi with his UNITA, into the forefront.

They began their operation by focussing the spotlight on Savimbi. Early in June 1974 Lisbon newspapers carried a prominently headlined report from Luanda saying that Savimbi intended to order UNITA troops to terminate military operations. Thereafter the Lisbon newspapers concentrated on Jonas Savimbi informing the readers about the course of the negotiations between him and the command of the Armed Forces in Angola. Here are a few excerpts from these reports:

Diário Popular, June 11. "The UNITA Secretary for Internal Affairs and member of its Central Committee, António Nicolau who also bears the name of António Vakulukuta declared: 'We have trust in the honest and serious intentions of the present Portuguese leaders'. Dr. Mario Soares suggested that negotiations with the UNITA might take place either in Portugal, Europe or Angola. Dr. António Nicolau disclosed that most of the weapons used by his movement had been seized from the Portuguese forces and that it also used the materiel captured from the MPLA in the battles with the members of this movement."

Diário de Noticias, June 13. "Luanda, June 12. At a press conference this evening General Franco Pinheiro said that the contacts which the Armed Forces established with Jonas Savimbi, UNITA 'leader' with the help of their liaison man, a Catholic priest, were 'most positive'. The Commander further declared: 'Now we have a basis for further work. We know Dr. Savimbi well and this is very important.' "

O Século, June 14. "Luanda. Addressing a press conference yesterday evening, General Franco Pinheiro described the contacts between the Armed Forces and Jonas Savimbi, leader of UNITA, which were established with the help of a Catholic priest, as most positive. Franco Pinheiro declared: 'Thus, in my opinion, the establishment of contacts has proved to be most useful because at least one of the leaders of the liberation movements told us what he was thinking about. Now we know more or less what he wants. Therefore we shall continue to move in this direction and I think that this will benefit democracy.' "

Diário de Lisboa, June 17. "There was a meeting between a group of [Portuguese–O.I.] officers and the UNITA leadership. The UNITA delegation included Jonas Savimbi, Major Tchapa, Captain Eduardo André, Captain Samuel Martinho Epalanga and Lieutenant Verissimo Sabino. The Portuguese side included Lieutenant-Colonel Fernando Passos Ramos, Major Pedro Cazarat Moreira Dias and Captain Benjamin Almeida."

Diário de Noticias, June 18. "The Portuguese Military Command in Angola and the UNITA have agreed to suspend military operations against each other. An official announcement to this effect was made this evening in Luanda [June 17–O. I.]. The Portuguese military mission was led by Colonel Passos Ramos, Chief of the Military Security Police which has a very good knowledge of the region where UNITA guerrillas operate. The communique underlined that a group of Portuguese officers will shortly fly to Lisbon to report on the course of the negotiations with UNITA to the Provisional Government. . . .

"... *UNITA is the smallest of the three guerrilla organisations operating in Angola. According to our estimates it has approximately 300 armed men in forests where there are practically no roads* [My italics–O. I.] in the central part of Eastern Angola."

I do not question the integrity of the Portuguese journalists who filed these reports. Most of them sincerely believed that a "cease-fire" agreement with one of the "national liberation movements" was a major achievement. That accounts for the fact that their reports sometimes unintentionally disclosed the backstage machinations in the dirty game that was going on in Angola. Indeed, how could anyone pay serious attention to a "liberation movement" numbering 300 fighters. Correspondents who hastened to interview the "intrepid Catholic priest", the liaison man between the Portuguese Command and Savimbi, described his "unsurpassed courage" in glowing terms. Just think of it, here was a man "who risked his life for the sake of peace" and entered the lion's den–the mysterious headquarters of Jonas Savimbi, the ferocious UNITA leader.

Here is one such account of the priest's adventures. "Beginning with April 25, a date which marked a happy turning point in events. . . Padre António de Araújo Oliveira of the St. Pedro and St. Paulo mission in Luso gave new forms to the existing contacts which he continues to maintain in absolute secrecy, but with the knowledge of the Armed Forces. On April 16 there was to be a meeting between him and Dr. Jonas Savimbi. But it did not take place because the letter setting the day of meeting arrived late. . . .

"The meeting between Padre Oliveira and Dr. Jonas Savimbi took place on April 28. Although we were not present at this meeting we know that it created a great impression on Padre Oliveira. He said that the UNITA leader had a very clear mind and that he creates the impression of being a very honest person. . . .

"'As regards us,' he declared: '. . . The past is dead and we can build nothing durable on its basis if we persist in our hatred for each other. . . .'

" '. . . Dr. Savimbi asks us for nothing more than recognition in Angola. . .' [My italics–O. I.].

". . . One thing is certain: for the first time a liberation movement in an overseas territory, based in Angola, with its 'leader' ceased fire on its own accord, although from the military point of view it had no need to do so. . . .

"Contacts will be continued and in my opinion they may lead up to negotiations at the highest level. . . ."

So, scorning the dangers that lay in wait for him the brave padre went into the unknown and achieved peace with "the national liberation movement of Dr. Jonas Savimbi". Moreover, and I would like to stress this, Savimbi's only request was to be recognised in Angola.

Sooner or later there comes a time, however, when true facts come to light. And that was exactly what happened with the "heroic" deed of Padre Oliveira. On October 22, 1975, almost a year and a half after the events which have been described above, the Angolan newspaper *Diário de Luanda* revealed the truth about the role played by Padre Oliveira, devoting a whole page to his adventures. Here is an excerpt from the article entitled *Sooner or Later the Truth Will Be Out.* "All of us remember that a month and a half after April 25 a communique was published which stated that UNITA was the first of the 'independence movements to sign a cease-fire agreement' and that it was reached thanks to the help of a certain Oliveira, a priest of the St. Pedro and St. Paulo parish in the city of Luso. And to make it easier for the public to swallow this concoction the communique was accompanied by an account of how the padre risked his life in order to achieve this agreement, that he did so for the general good, etc., etc. The purpose of all this was make the readers believe that contacts with . . . Malheiro Savimbi had only just been established by the padre. And all of us were convinced that Oliveira had actually played a major role in the establishment of peace in Angola. But this was far from true. Very far. . . ." To prove this the newspaper also published a letter. It was the seventh letter which I mentioned at the end of the preceding chapter.

Dated February 15, 1974 it was written by Padre António de Araújo Oliveira and addressed to the Secretary-General of the State of Angola Lieutenant-General Soares Carneiro who was subsequently involved in the attempted coup of

March 11, 1975 and locked up together with the other conspirators. (True, none of them were punished and were gradually and quietly released.)

Here is the text:

"Parish of St. Pedro and St. Paulo

"P. O. Box No. 120

"Luso, Angola.

"Luso, February 15, 1974

"To His Excellency Senhor Secretary General
of the State of Angola

"Luanda

"Your Excellency Senhor Secretary General

"My respectful compliments.

"I regret to have to take up your time which is so valuable to the service of the public cause. It has come to pass that in view of the circumstances and the results of the latest meeting with UNITA representatives (February 14, 1974), I find it absolutely necessary to approach Your Excellency with the sole aim of presenting my personal considerations and suggestions.

"All this should take place in the course of our personal meeting, since very often the thought is lost in a written report or at best the idea is expressed inadequately. It is my intention to give a most lucid account of all that has transpired in the course of the past negotiations in order to avoid any misunderstanding.

"1) I have set February 28 as the date for our next meeting. Dr. Savimbi will have to be present in person 'in order to advance with all possible speed' (I'm quoting from Savimbi's letter of February 10, 1974). He will expect us to make proposals. At the same time we expect him to make proposals... This accounts for my wish to receive instructions which I shall follow at the meeting.

"2) A question concerning the cease-fire. Are we really interested in it? On what conditions and what will its ultimate objective be? Perhaps simply to create conditions for serious negotiations?

"I realise that we shall discuss this problem and await the outcome of the current military campaign. But there is nothing to prevent us from talking on this subject because negotiations will start fifteen days from now and there is time to act in conformity with the outcome of the military operations now in progress.

"3) My personal efforts are evident from my letter to Dr. Savimbi of February 13, 1974. They are designed to dispel the coolness between us and also to convince him of our goodwill in achieving a peaceful termination of the conflict.

"4) I have even made so bold as to mention that it would be useful if Your Excellency would meet Dr. Savimbi. As I see it such a meeting will provide the only opportunity for reaching mutual understanding. May I at this time transmit that this is the wish of Your Excellency?

"The venue, date and security matters will be discussed later.

"5) I am making the most of my influence to persuade the UNITA to reduce the cruelties of this war to the minimum. So far at least they have proved to be gentlemen in fulfilling their promises. But they complain that sometimes there is no reciprocity on the part of our detachments. . . .

"Forgive me for the long letter. I, myself, am not satisfied with it, but I hope that eventually I will be in a position to give a personal account to Your Excellency. I can fly to Luanda by TAAG. This will be discreet and less expensive for the state budget.

Always at the service of your Excellency.

Respectfully, Padre António de Araújo Oliveira."

* * *

The Swedish information bulletin *Södra Africa* (No. 10, 1970) published the views of the prominent British Africa-watcher Basil Davidson concerning the tactic of "mountain topism". This term means that certain armed forces keep away from the struggle until victory is near. Then they come out from their hidings, involve themselves in the struggle and declare themselves as representatives of the people in order to be able to negotiate with the enemy, thus satisfying the interests of imperialism. This tactic was employed by neocolonialists and imperialists in Angola. Realising that neither Holden Roberto nor Jonas Savimbi were capable of independently assuming power in the country, they made every effort to bring the FNLA and UNITA in the forefront and thus be in a position to install people obedient to their will at the head of the future independent Angolan state.

There is another circumstance which should be borne in mind. At the initial stage of the revolution some senior Portuguese Army officers who aligned themselves with the Armed Forces Movement, had only a vague idea of the future of the colonies which Portugal had ruled for more than five centuries. Among them were people who firmly believed that Portugal should retain her hold over Angola. Typical in this respect were the views expressed by General Costa Gomes. In June 1974 when he was still Chief of the General Staff of the Portuguese Armed Forces he told a correspondent of *To the Point International*[1]: "I'm convinced that Angola will decide to remain Portuguese." When asked to comment on the request of the Angolan organisations that Portugal should sever diplomatic relations with South Africa and Rhodesia, he said: "Personally I regard the request illogical. We want to preserve relations with our friends. We do not want to sever our contacts. We want to strengthen them." When he became president of Portugal he changed his opinion, and when Angola became independent it was precisely Costa Gomes who signed the decree recognising the People's Republic of Angola.

Evidently Jonas Savimbi knew that such sentiments were current among a part of the senior officers of the Portuguese Army, and tried to go in step with them. On June 17, for example, the Lisbon newspaper *Diário de Notícias* published his letter dated June 9 advocating that Angolan independence should be preceded by a period of preparing her people for democratic life. It was very easy, he said, to demand immediate independence for Angola but first of all it was necessary to prepare the people for this act.

In a word the prospect for a swift decolonisation of Angola encountered vigorous resistance on the part of Portugal's Right-wing forces and their henchmen in Angola. One of the most diehard opponents of Angolan independence was the then President of Portugal General António de Spínola. From the day he assumed the post he was dead set against holding talks with PAIGC, FRELIMO and MPLA, the only movements in Guinea (Bissau), Mozambique and Angola which had struggled for many years against the

---

[1] *To the Point International* is a bi-weekly which is published by a Dutch company in both South African Republic and the Netherlands.– O. I.

Portuguese colonialists. Characteristic in this respect was a conversation which General Otelo Saraiva de Carvalho, one of the leaders of the Armed Forces Movement at the time, quotes in his book *Five Months which Changed Portugal*. This conversation took place between him and Spínola in the middle of 1974. After the first, preliminary negotiations with FRELIMO the then Foreign Minister Mário Soares and General Carvalho went to the Presidential Palace to report to General Spínola. "I clearly enunciated the conditions for decolonisation and referred to the position taken up by FRELIMO which in my opinion was the most correct and possible. General Spínola gave a jump. 'That won't do. There must be other solutions,' he shouted. 'Not a word more. It'll be best for you to keep quiet.' I bolstered my assertions with other arguments. 'We can prevent a rift between us and the future Mozambique,' I maintained, 'only if we come to an agreement with FRELIMO.' 'No senhor, that won't do,' he replied, 'because if the need arises, I, at my level, will approach Nixon and he will send American troops there.' I pointed out that this would entail a risk of Vietnamising the conflict in Mozambique, which, undoubtedly, was something that Nixon himself was not interested in. 'Well,' Spínola observed, 'if not Nixon, then South Africa will give us her troops.' "

It is important to note that this book was published in Lisbon in January 1975 when Spínola was no longer president, but still enjoyed all the privileges consistent with his rank and former position. Therefore, there is no reason whatsoever to doubt the authenticity of this dialogue. Comparing dates and events it can be assumed that it took place at the end of August 1974. And on September 14, Spínola had a meeting with General Mobutu.

The numerous journalists who accompanied Spínola on his trip had very little information about the course of the talks as can be judged from the report carried on September 16, 1974 by the Lisbon newspaper *O Século*:

"Spínola-Mobutu: Meeting on the Island of Sal.

"On Saturday, September 14, the President of the Republic António de Spínola met President of the Republic of Zaire General Mobutu on the Island of Sal to exchange views, particularly about the process of decolonisation of the Portuguese territory in Africa, which reportedly took place 'in an atmosphere of great cordiality'.

"The head of the Portuguese state, the Minister for Defence and Coordination of Territories Lieutenant-Colonel Firmino Miguel, Dr. Almeida Santos and members of the Military Chancellery and the Military and Civilian Cabinets arrived on the Island of Sal at 11.30 hours on an Air Force plane. President Mobutu arrived 45 minutes later. He was accompanied by the Chief of the Civilian Cabinet of the Head of the State of Zaire Bisengimana Rwena and adviser Bula Mandungo.

"After inspecting the Guard of Honour made up of an infantry unit and a paratrooper company, the two presidents and persons accompanying them went to Santa Maria Restaurant where at approximately 13.30 hours they sat down to luncheon which was also attended by the Military Commandant of the Island of Sal Lieutenant-Colonel António José dos Santos.

"At 15.00 hours the two heads of states began talks behind closed doors which lasted until 16.30 hours.

"After the talks, according to a France Press cable, President António de Spínola declared that the 'talks will produce good results in the future', and that his meeting with Mobutu made for 'a very friendly exchange of views concerning the process of decolonisation in Portuguese territories in Africa.'

"Unconstrained and smiling Generals Spínola and Mobutu signed the restaurant's distinguished guests' book and then went to the airport from where the Head of the State of Zaire flew to Dakar, capital of the Republic of Senegal.

"Before take off, according to France Press, Mobutu 'expressed his thanks for the warm welcome accorded him'. At the same time General Spínola expressed his satisfaction at the 'cordial atmosphere at the negotiations with the President of Zaire'. At parting the two presidents had a long handshake.

"President Mobutu's plane took off from the Island of Sal at about 17.15 hours. Shortly afterwards General Spínola and his entourage, with the exception of Minister Almeida Santos who left for Praia to preside over a session of the Municipal Council, flew to Lisbon.

"After the meeting of the two heads of state the following communique was handed out to the representatives of the press: 'The Presidents of the Republic of Zaire and Portugal met on the Island of Sal to exchange views. Inter alia they discussed the process of decolonisation currently taking place in Portugal's African territories.'·''

Anyone reading this dispatch will shrug his shoulders at the lack of information about the meeting itself. Naturally, the journalists tried to get hold of at least a few details and peep under the curtain of secrecy which shrouded the Spínola-Mobutu talks. The next day *O Século* reported: "The meeting on the Island of Sal was prepared during secret talks between Kinshasa and Lisbon. The last preparations were made after the arrival of a top-ranking officer of the Portuguese Army, a close associate of General Spínola, in Kinshasa. So, it was on the invitation from the President of the Portuguese Republic that President Mobutu went to the Island of Sal last Saturday."

And, of course, no one doubted that the future of Angola was discussed at the secret negotiations on the Island of Sal.

I was in Lisbon at the time and every morning I would go to the small bookshop in Restauradores Square to buy newspapers published in the Portuguese colonies which were delivered by air to the Portuguese capital. On September 17 late in the afternoon I purchased my daily bundle of Mozambique and Angolan newspapers, and one of them, the morning *A Provincia de Angola*, carried an item in large print which read: "The brevity of the communique was for us living here in Angola, like a cold shower descending on the head of a man sitting on a suitcase. . . . But the communique also contained concrete facts, particularly in the section where it was stated that General Spínola arrived in Sal in the company of Dr. Mário Soares, and that General Mobutu brought along Holden Roberto."

The Lisbon press did not report this fact. Neither was there any mention about Mário Soares and Holden Roberto in the communique which was published in the Lisbon newspapers and broadcast over radio and television. And yet this was a very eloquent fact.

The Spínola-Mobutu talks took place when attention in Luanda was focussed on the coming formation of a provisional government. On September 2, the Lisbon *O Seculo* wrote: "The provisional government will probably include a representative of the 'centre', engineer Fernando Falcão, President of FUA (United Front of Angola) who is well known in the country. . ., Jonas Savimbi's UNITA maintains very close ties with the moderates in the FUA which places its stake on UNITA."

Formally FUA was not a party and was regarded as a "voluntary organisation". In fact, however, the FUA was backed by all the financial big shots of Angola and the majority of the white settlers' parties which existed at the time, such as, for example, the Christian-Democratic Party of Angola (PCDA) headed by António Joaquim Ferronha and the Nationalist Union of Angola (UNA) led by engineer Angelino Alberto.

Several days after the Spínola-Mobutu talks it was announced in Luanda that a provisional government would be formed. It was also intimated that Fernando Falcão planned to become its deputy foreign minister.

Just then, fulfilling an assignment from the *Pravda*, I flew out of Lisbon to make a tour of Portugal's former colonies in Africa and remained in Luanda, capital of Angola, from September 18 to 24.

Here are a few pages from my *Angolan Diary* of that period.

September 18, 1974

The heavyweight Boeing-727 with a hundred passengers on board winged its way from Lisbon heading for the south of the African continent to Luanda, the capital of Angola, the largest and wealthiest Portuguese colony. It was a wearisome journey. It began on a plane of the Bermuda line but an hour or so later one of the engines failed. Luckily the other three didn't and we returned to Lisbon without mishap. Now we were on a TAP flight—a "domestic" Portuguese air company. The passengers were a bit tense and excited, either due to the unpleasant experience in the air, or in anticipation of what they will see in Angola. The situation there today, in the middle of September 1974, is, frankly speaking, complicated and there is no forecasting the events which might take place there, in the largest Portuguese colony, without taking stock of the situation on the spot.

Seated next to me is a thinnish man of forty with an anxious face. It is a long 10-hour trip to Luanda and one is bound to strike up an acquaintance with someone occupying the adjoining seat. I discovered that my neighbour was a CUCA employee. The CUCA group is a powerful monopoly controlled by Portuguese and foreign, as well as Angolan capital. There are more than 20 companies, mostly connected with food production, which are associated with CUCA. The man next to me works in CUCA's Lisbon office which is in charge of Angolan factories manufacturing beer and soft drinks. He has relatives in Luanda and in order to bring them back to Lisbon with him has persuaded his manager to send him on a business trip to Angola.

"You know, after reading the newspaper my hair seems to stand on end from the very thought of what is going to happen there, in Angola. I'm a humble man and very far from politics. But let me tell you that if we pull out of Angola she will become a scene of carnage. I hope to get my old folks, my father's brother and sister, out of the country before this happens. But I'm worried about getting return tickets. I've heard that all seats right up to the end of the year have been booked. Perhaps you know someone in TAP?"

I told him that I knew no one in TAP and that it was my first visit to the capital of Angola. He sighed, moved uneasily in his seat, adjusted its back at a convenient angle and dosed off, evidently deciding to forget his worries. It was four in the morning and there was time to get some rest before the plane landed in Luanda....

"Where are you from, senhor?" The policeman in Luanda airport glanced with curiosity at the pages of my passport endorsed with numerous visas.

"From the Soviet Union."

"Do you mean that you're a Soviet citizen? I've been here for thirty years and you're the first Soviet person I've let in." Breathing on the rubber stamp he impressed an entry mark on my passport and handed it back, saying: "Have a pleasant stay in the capital of our Angola."

The capital of Angola has two totally unlike parts, and while they form a single whole they exist independently of each other. From a plane circling Luanda one gets a good view of the blue waters of the ocean, a segment of the coast with modern, European-type buildings most of which are white, and right next to them thousands of hovels, huts and barracks.

The modern part of the city (called "down town") is inhabited by the white settlers, numbering about 150,000. The slums, or *musseques*, are the home of approximately half a million Africans and mullatoes. The existence of the down town and the *musseques* in Luanda exposed the utter absurdity of Salazar's propaganda which claimed that there was no racial discrimination in the Portuguese colonies.

Upon entering a country where there is no Soviet Embassy or Consulate (and not a single Soviet person, for that matter), the first thing to do is to visit the local authorities. In those days a Government Council headed by the Lisbon-appointed Chairman Vice-Admiral Alva Rosa Coutinho was in charge of all affairs in Angola. Angola was just entering the initial period of the completion of decolonisation. The term "initial period of completion" is fairly accurate because the country has been fighting for her independence since 1961.

I knew no one in Luanda and before departing I studied tourist guides of the city which were available in my Lisbon hotel and decided to stop at Hotel Globo. According to plan it was almost in the centre of the city and, the guidebook said, it was a fairly inexpensive place.

September 19

Hotel Globo was a modest affair even for Africa. The receptionist who was also the porter offered to show me rooms and pick the one I liked best. Evidently there were not too many people living in the hotel. Leaving my belongings in the room and taking along my camera "just in case" I went downstairs in search of newspapers and to find out where the Government Council had its offices. There had to be someone who would look after and help foreign correspondents in the country. When I came up to the receptionist's desk he was inspecting the police card I had filled in upon arrival.

"So you're a Soviet journalist? You've come to take a look at the goings on in Angola?"

"Yes, I'll try to get my bearings, if that's possible."

"We're at a loss ourselves. I've heard that there was an officers' meeting at the governor's palace the day before yesterday. They came not only from nearby garrisons, but virtually from all Angolan towns. No one knows what went on there. And today there'll be a meeting of the Christian-Democratic Party of Angola, the PCDA, senhor Ferronha's party. It's all in the papers." He handed me a copy of *A Provincia de Angola* and said: "We've also been hearing that FNLA detachments, Senhor Holden Roberto's detachments, are advancing on Luanda. But so many rumours are afloat that one doesn't know what to believe."

I took the newspaper, asked the way to the former gubernatorial palace and went out into Salvador Correia Street. A thirty minutes' walk through the centre of the city would take me from the hotel to the hill where the palace stood. I was amased by the large number of posters which covered house walls and lampposts and were even stuck on car windshields. There were MPLA posters bearing Agostinho Neto's photograph and some FNLA posters. But most of the posters had been put up by UNITA and FUA.

The palace's main entrance was sentried by two Portuguese soldiers who paid absolutely no attention to the people who entered the building. After roaming the corridors I finally located an office, where I was told that the Chairman of the Council Vice-Admiral Alva Rosa Coutinho had left for Lisbon by plane this morning but that I would be received by the Chief of his Cabinet, Captain 2nd Class Jorje Correia Jesuino (subsequently he held the post of Minister of Public Means of Communication and Information in the fifth provisional government of Portugal). He received me very cordially and willingly described the situation in Angola, particularly in Luanda, giving a detailed account of the difficulties which faced the country. He said that most of these difficulties were of a political nature and stemmed from the tangled knot of interests of various internal groups plus backstage intrigues conducted by forces connected with the imperialist monopolies, or South African racialists.

"Unfortunately," he observed, "in view of my post it would be improper for me to characterise to a foreign correspondent the numerous organisations and parties which we have today in Angola. But I'll instruct our Information Department to help organise a series of meetings with local politicians and they will bring you up to date on the course of events."

I requested the Captain to help me with accreditation and asked him about the formalities I should observe in order to attend the meeting which, according to the newspaper, the PCDA was holding today.

It turned out that in the current situation accreditation was unnecessary and that as far as he knew anyone could be present at the meeting.

The chief of the cabinet ordered his "press sector" to help me contact a leader of the Democratic Movement of Angola (MDA).

Within an hour after meeting Senhor Jorje Correia Jesuino I was in conversation with a leader of the MDA. Two West German TV correspondents also went along for the sake of "ideological balance" as it were.

The MDA is the largest and most representative legal organisation established by democratic forces in Angola after April 25, 1974. It has branches in all Angolan towns and unites tens of thousands of people, the local intelligentsia, the petty and middle bourgeoisie and students, mostly white settlers.

Antonio Cardoso, an MDA leader, received us in the editorial offices of the weekly *ABC-Diário de Angola* because the MDA leadership did not disclose the whereabouts of its headquarters to strangers.

He explained that the MDA was established for the purpose of disseminating and elucidating the aims and tasks of the MPLA. The fact of the matter was that the MPLA had no official representatives in Luanda and other towns, pending official permission from the Portuguese authorities, and its aims and tasks were explained by the MDA and another organisation—the National African League (LNA) which was active among the country's African population.

"The MDA," said Antonio Cardoso, "operates in very complicated conditions. We experience great material difficulties and are unable, for example, to put out propaganda material. Moreover, Right- and ultra Right-wing groups of parties and organisations have unleashed a campaign of terror against all MPLA supporters. A large number of Right-wing organisations which appeared literally within days after April 25 are active in Angola. What do you know about FUA, UNA, MOPUA, MDIA and PSDA? I'll wager that all these names are a meaningless combination of letters for you. And yet they are names of 'parties' and 'movements' angling for a piece of the Angolan pie. Here's another name, FLEC. You're aware, of course, that extremely rich deposits of oil which are being developed by Gulf Oil have been discovered in the Angolan enclave of Cabinda. Well, FLEC has been set up on Gulf Oil funds and has proclaimed that it is working for the secession of Cabinda from Angola.

"Here's another example. Even two. FUA stands for Front for the Unity of Angola. Its head is the industrial and financial magnate Fernando Falcão. Naturally, FUA's aims have nothing in common with our interests. Its leadership dreams of implementing the Rhodesian version of independence in Angola, but intends to bring several 'obedient' Africans into the government for the sake of camouflage.

"The leadership of another white organisation, MOPUA, includes a large number of former agents of Salazar's PIDE and people who had collaborated with it. MOPUA stands for Popular Movement for Angolan Unity. Just imagine, they call themselves a 'popular movement' and even fighters for 'unity' while in effect the organisation is simply a rostrum for former PIDE agents and informers. Naturally, these organisations were set up here, in Angola, after the overthrow of fascism in Portugal not to support the national liberation movement of our people, but to seize command posts and thus be in a position to prevent those who really express the interests of the Angolan people, from coming to power.

"Perhaps you'll be interested to know that there are three terroristic racialist organisations in Luanda. Their names have already appeared on the walls of some houses. They are FRA, RUA and ESINA. The members of these gangs instigated riots and assassinations in Luanda in May and June. These thugs are very closely connected with South African racialists and fascist elements in Angola herself, and their aim is to kill the leaders of progressive Angolan organisations."

He asked us not to mention his name and not because he was overcautious. Several days ago the RUA bandits attempted to kill him by firing at him as he was driving into the city. They sprayed the car with submachine-gun fire but luckily he was not hit. The West German TV correspondents asked whether they could photograph one of the sittings of the MDA Steering Committee.

"Yes," he replied, "but you mustn't photograph our faces. We'll pick you up and drive you to the building where our meeting will be held."

Comrade Cardoso, I should like to say, was no coward. During fascist rule severe trials fell to his lot and he passed them with honour. He had served 13 years in Salazar's and Caetano's prisons and concentration camps. He spent three years in the Tarrafal concentration camp from which he was released after April 25, 1974, five months prior to our meeting.

I was back at the hotel at about five in the afternoon. To my surprise there was a long line of suitcases of all sizes at the entrance, and dust-covered cars which evidently had covered many hundreds of kilometres were parked at the curb.

Spotting me the receptionist smiled and said: "You were lucky, senhor journalist. If you arrived only just now I would have no room to offer you. There are so many arrivals, so many of them, and all from the north, from the northern provinces. Refugees I would say. It looks as though the end of the world has arrived."

I found out that FNLA detachments began entering the small towns in the northern provinces bordering on Zaire, and the Portuguese garrisons in these towns showed absolutely no concern. The FNLA gave no indication yet of whether its intentions were good or bad. People who tried to find that out drew a blank because none of the men in FNLA uniform knew either Portuguese or any of the local dialects. That was why many of the inhabitants preferred to abandon their homes. Those who had cars packed them with belongings, while the poorer folk collectively hired buses, formed a column and headed for Luanda, away from misfortunes that might descend upon them.

In the evening I went to the PSDA meeting. It took place in a building called Mutamba, which, I gathered, was the party's headquarters. There was a fairly large turnout, about fifteen hundred people, or more, very few of whom were Africans.

As a matter of fact it was not even a party meeting, but something in the nature of a rally at which the PSDA enunciated its position and explained how it visualised the Angola's future. It was interesting to hear the speech of the General Secretary of the Party António Ferronha, particularly that part of it in which he spoke of his party's attitude to various organisations and movements in Angola. Well, he did not even mention the MPLA, as though it did not even exist. But he was most generous in praising the 'merits' of Jonas Savimbi and the UNITA. *He declared that the PSDA maintains close contacts with the UNITA, particularly with Jonas Savimbi, who was his personal friend for many years, ever since their meeting in Kinshasa.*

Although it was very late when I returned to the hotel, I

decided to glance through the evening newspaper *O Comércio*. It frontpaged an account of yesterday evening's meeting of the FUA where Fernando Falcão announced its reorganisation into a party and said that his party (which will also be called FUA) intends to unite representatives of all ideological trends, with the exception of the extremists. He pointed out that the party was created in order to give all the Angolans a common political foundation and thus offer a real alternative to the liberation movements. At a press conference after the meeting Falcão said that for a long time to come no one party would be strong enough to win the majority. Therefore it was necessary to form a coalition government. He mentioned that he had already contacted some liberation groups and emphasised that *Jonas Savimbi was his best friend.*

What is interesting and significant is that the chiefs of the out-and-out reactionary parties vie with each other in publicising their friendship with the PIDE agent Jonas Savimbi. Evidently they have great hopes in the UNITA and believe that if rightly handled Jonas Savimbi can help them come to power.

September 20

Today I went to present myself to the editorial staff of *A Provincia de Angola* whose offices were almost next door to my hotel. At first Assistant Chief Editor Senhor Sarmiento, an old man of 65, who received me, seemed a bit frightened, evidently unprepared for a conversation with a Soviet journalist. But I put him at ease by saying that my visit was more in the nature of protocol. "I am terribly sorry," he said, "but I'm not authorised to discuss politics and the Chief Editor Senhor Ruy Correia Freitas is out of town." It was a disappointing visit.

When I was having lunch at the hotel restaurant the receptionist came up and said that I was wanted on the phone. The caller was João Morais, a member of the board of the organisation which Comrade Antonio Cardoso mentioned during yesterday's meeting at the editorial offices of the *ABC* journal.

He said that he would pick me up and take me to the *Angola* journal put out by the National African League.

I saw a copy of this journal with a photograph of Agostinho Neto on the cover in the MDA offices. This was an indication of the journal's orientation.

Morais was punctual and after a short drive we pulled up at a two-storyed building situated in Conde Ficalho Street in the southeastern part of Luanda. The premises, outwardly resembling either a club or a theatre, were owned by the National African League. It had a conference hall on the first floor and rooms for exhibitions and various study circles on the second, and also housed the editorial offices of the League's journal *Angola*.

The League was founded forty odd years ago and all that time was fully controlled by the fascist authorities which tried to spread their influence to the country's African population with the help of trusted elements. After fascism was overthrown in Portugal the henchmen of the old regime were immediately expelled from the League and its new democratic leadership concentrated on turning it into a cultural centre serving the cause of Angola's independence.

We arrived at the League when there was a debate in progress among young people on the subject "the role of Angolan national independence movements in the current process of the country's decolonisation". I heard some of the speakers. Their speeches were temperamental and passionate but, unfortunately, some speakers had only a superficial knowledge of the history of the national liberation struggle.

Later Morais confirmed Antonio Cardoso's words that the League wholly supports the MPLA. "But," he added, "there are people who still have not found their bearings in the situation and have come under the influence of the FNLA and UNITA propaganda. We organise extensive discussions at which we enunciate the programme, aims and tasks of the MPLA and relate the history of the struggle."

Returning to my hotel late in the evening the Chief Editor of *Angola* and I saw a car stop on Brito Godins Avenue near the centre of the city. Three men, definitely not Africans, got out and began sticking large posters on the façade of the nearest building. There was a streetlight nearby and we saw a half-length portrait of Jonas Savimbi above an inscription which read: "Only Savimbi and the UNITA express the true aspirations of the people of Angola."

September 22

Today's issue of *A Provincia de Angola* devoted almost half a page to a statement put out by Fernando Falcão's FUA in connection with a meeting of the Portuguese Army officers in Angola which took place on September 18. I had heard about this meeting from the receptionist at Hotel Globo on the day of my arrival.

The FUA statement said that 500 officers of all three branches of the Portuguese Armed Forces gathered at the gubernatorial palace in Luanda on September 18 to work out a stand concerning Angola's future. The meeting decided that only people who had fought against the colonialists arms in hand constituted the sole political force which had the right to speak in behalf of the Angolan people. The FUA categorically disagreed. It demanded that the political parties in Angola which came into being after April 25 should be allowed to participate in resolving questions connected with the future decolonisation of Angola and in the administration of the country.

Today I witnessed the beginning of a mass campaign by white settlers in support of the UNITA. About a dozen pickups which were being loaded with posters bearing Savimbi's portrait and slogans demanding the transfer of power to the UNITA, were parked in front of a printshop owned by CUF, the most powerful Portuguese monopoly in the country. And by evening the entire central part of the town was plastered with them.

The evening paper *Diário de Luanda* reported that Holden Roberto's FNLA units had passed through Carmona and three detachments occupied a number of barracks abandoned by Portuguese troops in the middle of September. The paper also continued printing a series of laudatory articles about UNITA and Savimbi. There were also items "refuting" the facts which were reported by *Afrique-Asie* proving that Savimbi with his organisation was working for the Portuguese troops and that in its operations against the MPLA the UNITA used weapons delivered by the Portuguese military intelligence to Savimbi. On the opposite page, next to these items the paper carried a lengthy commentary whose author tried to prove that the MPLA was weak and ineffective.

All this shows that the situation in Angola continues to deteriorate and that the process of decolonisation preceding the proclamation of independence will prove to be extremely complicated. The Right-wing forces will never part with Angola just like that. I'm sure that the country is on the verge of a serious political and perhaps even a military crisis.

At daybreak on September 26 a group of 23 Angolans left Luanda by air for Lisbon at the invitation of Spínola to attend a meeting which was to begin on the same day. Among them were General Secretary of the Christian-Democratic Party of Angola António Ferronha, President of the Nationalist Union of Angola Angelino Alberto, representative of the so-called Front for the Liberation of Cabinda André Rodrigues Mingas and journalist Ruy Correia Freitas, all of whom were notorious for their extreme Rightist views. The others in the group were no better. After meeting Spínola all of them returned to Luanda on the following day, September 27.

It will be recalled that there was an attempted Right-wing state coup in Lisbon on September 28. The coup failed and Spínola was forced to resign his post. But the reactionary forces did not confine their actions to Portugal alone. Right-wing forces in Angola intended to launch an armed uprising with the view to turning Angola into an "independent state" under a white administration, which was to have taken place simultaneously with a planned demonstration of the "silent majority" in Lisbon.

In an interview to *A Província de Angola*, Admiral Alva Rosa Coutinho said that the coup had been planned by the Christian-Democratic Party. The party had a solid financial basis and intended to recruit soldiers, commandos and former PIDE agents, and send weapons to its supporters in Luanda. After the abortive coup "Jonas Savimbi's personal friend" the party's president Ferronha decamped to the South African Republic. The director of *A Província de Angola* Ruy Correia Freitas also dropped out of sight. Both men, as we know, were among the 23 Angolans whom General Spínola had summoned to Lisbon for talks.

General Spínola resigned on September 30. But his plans concerning Angola were set in motion and the Right-wing forces had no intention of cancelling them. In the evening of the day when Spínola handed in his resignation, the FUA leader Fernando Falcão flew from Luanda to Kinshasa on a plane which had been sent by the President of Zaire. Reporting this the France Press agency noted: "According to information coming from persons close to FUA, Fernando Falcão will establish contacts with FNLA leaders and possibly with Daniel Chipenda. Taking into account the very close relations between Falcão and UNITA President Savimbi it can also be concluded that the Zaire capital will become the venue of important talks on the future united political front which will serve as the basis for an independent Angola."

A book by Fernando Barciela Santos entitled *Angola– Dramatic Hour of Decolonisation* published in Lisbon in 1975 has the following lines: "At the end of September Holden Roberto's soldiers began to cross the Angola frontier en masse at the north. It looked as though the Mobutu-Spinola talks on the Island of Sal began to yield results. . . .

". . . On October 1 there was already talk about the threat of a white counter-revolution. MPLA Chairman Agostinho Neto asserted that South African advisers were organising a militia from among the white settlers in camps situated in the south of the country. He declared that three parties were directly involved: the PCD (Christian-Democratic Party), FUA (Front for the Unity of Angola) and the FRA (Angolan Resistance Front). . . .

". . . Details were vague, but as regards the main trends, the situation was fairly clear.

"Can one regard it as a coincidence that this movement [FNLA–O. I.] with its widely advertised anti-communist ideology and North American support undertook its strategic offensive into the northern part of Angola in the days preceding September 28?

"Today, too, no one doubts that the sole purpose of the strange meeting between Spínola and Mobutu on the Island of Sal was to turn Angola over to the FNLA. Spínola's right-wing views and his defence of the interests of the capitalists were incompatible with the idea that such a radical movement as the MPLA would gain the upper hand in Angola. His rejection of the earlier idea of a federation between Portugal and her colonies by no means signified that he was disposed to lose the whole game. . . ."

Basically, I agree with the assessment given by the author in these excerpts. But at the time neither Barciela Santos nor anyone else, not counting the handful of people who were directly involved in the conspiracy, had even the faintest inkling of the details of the talks which took place on the Island of Sal. The fact that these talks pursued far-reaching objectives was disclosed later, in an article headlined "Report on the Mobutu-Spínola Agreement" carried by *Diário de Luanda* on October 21, 1975. Here is an excerpt from this

said that it v
hoodlums us
sions I went
fire from FN
wrecked shai
In July 1
In France, h
sation with
Claude Pierr
henchmen cc
carried a rep
that it "indu
torture of pi
say: "I perse
no British ne
soners with
June 1975 th
MPLA prison
of Luanda. V
prisoners wer
All this to
Holden Rober
who promise
prising, there
UNITA chief
through a pol
On July 2.
against the N
so. On Septei
an article by
ceived an ali
France with
same August
he discussed
ments into th
the Johannesb
which many v
In Luanda
Dr. Dieter Co
like most corp
pedant in my
formation whi
agency. The A

tas, former director of *A Pro*
preceding Provisional Gov
Coutinho had mounted a hur
returned to Luanda and rest
Provincia de Angola. He mai
erty and enjoys the protectioi
disappeared from Luanda.

"Another fascist Jaime de
tor, has also returned to Luai
Information Department."

Let us recall what John Ma
berto purchasing the daily *A*
also recall that the group of
cent who visited Lisbon severa
counter-revolutionary coup in
Spinola also included Ruy Cor
of *A Provincia de Angola*. W
again becomes the director of
become Holden Roberto's prope

Here is another example ill
on which the FNLA chief relied
one of his numerous interviews
to the western journalists who h
his henchman Daniel Chipend
great fighter and a great patriot,
to point to his qualities inherent
ous patriot and a staunch fight
sion to join our movement and
and its programme of action are
found deliberation."

Six months later, when I was i
western correspondents who wer
voli and were in contact with ti
the various splitter groups, that C
dered the occupied Angolan tov
searched the abandoned enterpri
open their safes. Several months
the FNLA and UNITA and their
ing to the borders of Namibia and
Chipenda had bolted, with a vast
this connection the Luanda news
noted: "Being a traitor of his pe
Chipenda performed the finest pie

article: "The talks concerned the future which the two heads of state intended to prepare for Angola, for her people and her natural wealth. The meeting was held at the special invitation of Spinola. Each side presented its demands and defended its position.

"In the first place General Mobutu asked Spinola to support Holden Roberto in Angola separated from its Cabinda Province. In the second place he made the condition that Angola should be controlled jointly by Spinola's and Mobutu's men, and that Cabinda with its vast resources of oil should, on the other hand, be administered by people from the so-called Front for the Liberation of the Enclave of Cabinda with headquarters in Kinshasa. In turn these people would take orders from Spinola and Mobutu. In the third place, Spinola would help Mobutu create what he called a federation of Zaire-Angola-Cabinda with Mobutu as president and Holden Roberto as vice-president.

"These were the three points which Mobutu presented at the talks. Spinola accepted them but on his own conditions.

"First, Mobutu was to assist Spinola's men by putting in a word for them with a number of African leaders in order diplomatically to vindicate the Portuguese Government on the international scene and lend an appearance of respectability to Spinola himself by enabling him to take advantage of an opportunity which he would get to pursue a new colonial policy, and take steps to restore order inside Portugal. . . .

"Spinola also demanded that Mobutu should guarantee that all Portuguese and multinational companies operating in Angola under Portugal's protection should be able freely to dispose of the immense natural resources of Angola, Cabinda and Zaire for at least the next twenty years. Mobutu accepted this demand, too. . . ."

Later, the French *Le Monde* characterising the situation that had taken shape in Angola after September 1974 and quoting the views of some Lisbon leaders concerning Portugal's stand wrote that Portuguese neutrality in Angola was ambiguous. In the opinion of these leaders, the paper went on to say, Portuguese neutrality "favours the partner who is the most powerful in the military respect and who has the biggest external support, that is, the FNLA headed by Holden Roberto, to the detriment of Agostinho Neto's MPLA. . . .

105

"... Right up to S(
sonally concerned hi

"... In the opinior
secret talks with Nixo
to 'slow down' decol
Dr. Agostinho Neto's
believe that the 'polic
and Caetano was subtl
ticularly beginning w
miral Rosa Coutinho..

Thus, Right-wing el
conspiracies and althou
mained in force.

In the spring of 197
besides MPLA detachr
were also in Luanda, tl
tage the work of the
launched military operat
population of the capita
Affairs journal John Ma
April 1975 as follows: '
FNLA troops that had
companied by some ele
units in Luanda... Hold
est daily *A Provincia d*
and tried to implant his
da was the MPLA's bai
FNLA intrusion. As milit
some 50 MPLA militant
FNLA soldiers. ..."

In the FNLA headquart
cupied by its functionarie
were billeted one could 1
notorious fascists who ha
gime and former PIDE ag
all in getting all it wants
wrote Arslan Humbaraci
problem in his account of
days. "At the same time th
hibited the MPLA to use .
criminals of all calibres, pa
for PIDE had returned to /
of the FNLA, Humbaraci

ree
trai
his
Rol
S
terr
E
Sou
Afri
age
grea
peri
selv
Jona
supi
E
and
rank
Frer
Gen
Bros
der-S
Joan
W
UNI
orga
MPL
L'Hu
kille
In th
parti
week
by tl
ernm
Simp
the s
again
In '
of th
pses
One
holste
conne

gola and I read many of his reports after I had already re-turned to Moscow. In one of them he gave an account of his trip to the south of the country after the expulsion of UNITA bands from there. He wrote that he saw mutilated bodies littered around 20 mass graves at a jail near Bie, formerly Silva Porto. The number of corpses, he pointed out, could not be ascertained and added that he found 235 pairs of canvas shoes at the edge of a nearby maize field. "The prisoners must have had to take them off before they were killed," he wrote. "The last prisoners at the jail had been executed by UNITA soldiers shortly before the town was captured by the MPLA." According to his report UNITA members murdered 124 people at another prison at Rio Cuito near N'Zau Puna, and "further mass graves have been found near the airport at Huambo". An MPLA fighter, 24-year-old Domingos told him that 679 out of 720 detainees at a former UNITA base at Capolo, 70 kilometres from Bie, perished during their seven-month incarceration.

After being driven out of Bie and other towns, UNITA bands rolled back to the south, towards the Republic of South Africa. But that did not prevent Savimbi's men in various capitals from continuing to make boastful declarations. On January 23 UNITA "foreign minister" Sangumba declared in Lusaka that his organisation would continue to score victories with the help of the United States (!). Many western politicians took such statements seriously. One of them was US Senator Clark. Replying to a journalist who asked him who could best govern Angola, the Senator said that he personally had no doubt that none was better suited to play this role than Jonas Savimbi. He referred to the leader of the Portuguese Socialist Party Mário Soares who was in Washington at the time and who according to the Senator also believed that Dr. Savimbi could fill the role of Angola's leader better than anyone else.

These statements were made at a time when Roberto and Savimbi had just ended another visit to France and Britain, a visit which aroused the indignation of public opinion in these countries. Returning to Lusaka Savimbi met a representative of a West German Fund Friedrich Ebert. He also had a meeting with Roy Innis, one of the leaders of the US Congress of Racial Equality, and discussed with him details concerning the transportation of US mercenaries to Angola. But the days of the FNLA and UNITA were numbered.

The criminal existence of these CIA and PIDE agents, of these obedient tools of South African racists and western imperialist circles was coming to an end. At a meeting in Nova Lisboa in the beginning of October 1975 Savimbi with his usual aplomb told his supporters: "The MPLA can enter Huambo, it can enter Bie, but by then Savimbi will no longer be alive.... If UNITA loses Nova Lisboa it will die. And since we have no desire to die, the MPLA will not pass." But the MPLA entered Nova Lisboa and other towns and cleansed the territory of Angola of the scum that had infested it.

The giant aid in weapons, ammunition and manpower worth many millions went down the drain. In November 1975 the British weekly *West Africa* carried an editorial which quoted Savimbi as saying: "You will be really surprised at who is helping us." The ensuing chapters treat of the forces which nourished, encouraged and supported Holden Roberto, Jonas Savimbi and their bands.

Chapter V

Peking Enters the Game

Early in December 1963 Kenya was preparing solemnly to proclaim her independence, and foreign guests were arriving in Nairobi for the occasion. On December 10 a Chinese delegation led by Vice-Premier of the PRC State Council and Foreign Minister Marshal Chen Yi landed at Nairobi Airport. On the same day it was received by the future president of Kenya Jomo Kenyatta.

On December 12 tens of thousands of Kenyans packed the Uhuru stadium where a mass meeting marking the proclamation of independence was held. Foreign delegations occupied the stands reserved for distinguished guests. After the march past of the heroic detachments of the Mau Mau fighters who had emerged from the jungle after years of struggle and when the performances of amateur ensembles were drawing to a close Tom Mboya followed by an African sporting dark glasses approached the head of the Chinese delegation.

"Our dear Chinese friend," said Mboya to Chen Yi, "may I introduce our guest, the head of the Angolan Revolutionary Government in Exile Holden Roberto."

Turning around Tom Mboya made a gesture inviting Roberto to come up.

"Yes, I've heard about your government and your noble struggle," said Chen Yi smiling broadly. "It is a pleasure to make the acquaintance of such an outstanding African leader."

"Could you, Mr. Marshal," began Roberto groping for English words, "spare me a few minutes some day during your stay here? I would have. . ."

"Perhaps you'll find it easier to speak French?" interrupted Chen Yi. "I've lived in France and know the language."

"Oh yes, merci," Holden exclaimed and sinking his head into his shoulders he repeated his request.

"Come to the hotel where our delegation is staying tomorrow, at about eight. I'll leave instructions to have you admitted," Chen Yi replied and offered his hand which Holden respectfully shook.

On December 13 Holden Roberto was received in the suite of the head of the Chinese delegation where he talked for more than an hour with Chen Yi, the head of the West Asian and African Department of the Chinese Foreign Ministry Wang Yu-tien and other Chinese representatives who arrived in Kenya for the festivities. During the meeting Roberto was assured of Chinese aid and cooperation and Chen Yi suggested that Roberto should select people and sent them to Peking for training.

"I've carefully examined all the information about your activity which we have at our disposal," Chen Yi said, "and can say not only on my own behalf but also on behalf of the Chinese Government that we have many points of contact. I frankly admit that knowing the platforms of the other organisations working for Angolan independence, I regard your policy of not entering into alliances and forming any sort of a front with them as being quite realistic. You have set up a government in exile and enjoy the support of the government of the country where it has its seat at present, something which cannot be said about the other organisations. Moreover, your government has been recognised by the recently established Organisation of African Unity as the sole national liberation movement in Angola.

"Naturally, in the future we shall also receive other Angolan nationalist organisations, but that must cool your ardour. Our sympathies are with you. Of course, our conversation is strictly confidential and I hope that you won't breathe a word about it for otherwise our contacts will cease immediately. Soon we'll have an embassy here and then you'll communicate with its staff and also directly with the Ambassador."

That was how Roberto established contact with Peking in 1963. Subsequently, he often went to Nairobi and called at the Chinese Embassy in Wood Land Street. The fact of the matter was that for many years China did not have a diplomatic mission in Kinshasa so that Roberto simply had to make these trips to the Kenyan capital.

Soon the GRAE foreign minister Jonas Savimbi went to Peking for military training.

Later, when GRAE had been thrown out of the OAU and deprived of all financial aid, and when it was proclaimed that the MPLA was the sole legitimate representative of the Angolan people and the only national liberation movement fighting against the Portuguese colonialists in the country, Peking lost much of its interest in Roberto and his government. The relations between China and Holden Roberto revived somewhat in 1973 when the Chipenda-led splitter group in the MPLA tried to counterpose itself to its legitimate leadership headed by Agostinho Neto.

On November 25, 1972 Peking and Kinshasa officially normalised relations and early in January 1973 President Mobutu of Zaire accompanied by Holden Roberto set out by plane on an official tour of Asian countries which was highlighted by a visit to Peking. On Monday, January 29, Kung Te-fei, the first Chinese Ambassador in Zaire, assumed his duties in Kinshasa. Several days later Holden Roberto was presented to him.

But it was after April 25, 1974, the day when fascism fell in Portugal, that China's relations with Roberto's bands began to flower in the full sense of the word. Early in May Ambassador Kung Te-fei had a confidential conversation in the presidential palace. It lasted for two hours and was also attended by Holden Roberto. The next day Peking received a long coded account of the conversation from the Chinese Embassy in Zaire. In the main it dealt with proposals concerning aid to Roberto's organisation.

In the last week of May Peking gave a send off to a group of Chinese military instructors bound for Africa. Two of the senior officers heading the group bound for Zaire were received by the PRC Prime Minister. On June 3 the group arrived in Kinshasa and on the following day the Lisbon *A Capital* newspaper published a France Press cable from Kinshasa under the headline "Holden Roberto Receives Chinese Instructors", which said: "FNLA President Holden Roberto has received in his headquartes the first contingent of Chinese instructors, all specialists in guerrilla warfare. A communique was published which said that the meeting took place in a 'very cordial' atmosphere.... The Chinese instructors headed by a Political Commissar and a Divisional General conveyed to Holden Roberto and all FNLA fighters 'warm

114

congratulations' from the leaders of the Chinese people and reassured them, the communique underlined, that people's China was firmly determined to support the struggle of the Angolan people against Portuguese colonialism until final victory.

"The communique also said that in reply President Holden Roberto thanked the leaders of the Chinese Republic for their favourable response to FNLA's request to send Chinese instructors to train fighters for the army of national liberation."

On June 5 another Lisbon paper, *O Seculo*, wrote that according to a representative of the Portuguese Armed Forces the arrival on Saturday of instructors placed by the Chinese Government at the disposal of the FNLA in Kinshasa did not come as a surprise to military observers in Luanda who knew about their forthcoming arrival and were expecting it.

Thus, a fairly paradoxical and at first glance incomprehensive situation began to take shape. Forty days had already passed since the overthrow of the fascist regime in Portugal. The new democratic authorities unequivocally proclaimed the beginning of a new era in the country's relations with African nations which were still under Portuguese rule. Portuguese officers and soldiers firmly refused to conduct military operations against the national liberation movements in Guinea (Bissau), Mozambique and Angola and demanded to be transported back to Portugal. But at the very same time a group of more than 100 Chinese military instructors arrived in Kinshasa and, according to Roberto's declaration, would start raising an FNLA army. Why was it necessary to raise this army if Holden Roberto's detachments were inactive when the Portuguese colonialists ruled the country? Against whom the FNLA detachments, which were being formed and trained by the Chinese and whose activation Holden Roberto had announced, would be used?

Definitely not against the Portuguese units still stationed in Angola. It was clear from numerous statements by Portuguese military that Portugal would no longer fight in Angola. New Portugal was resolved to withdraw from Angola as quickly as possible. The only organised, trained and disciplined force that remained in the country were the detachments of the Popular Movement for the Liberation of Angola (MPLA). And it was against them that Roberto's units, which the Chinese were hastily raising, would have to fight.

The 11th Session of the Assembly of Heads of African States and Governments—Members of the Organisation of African Unity opened in Mogadiscio on July 12, 1974. It was attended by all the 42 members of the organisation the majority of whom were represented by their presidents. Naturally, the main item on the agenda was the national liberation struggle with the situation in the Portuguese colonies coming under the heaviest scrutiny. At this concluding sitting the Assembly passed a resolution proclaiming its all-round support for the struggle in territories under Portuguese rule.

Holden Roberto, that "fighter for freedom", was also in the capital of Somalia in those days. He offered the journalists to interview him, posed for photographs, and in general tried to attract attention to his person. Here is what a France Press correspondent wrote in a cable which was published by the Mozambique newspaper *A Noticias da Beira* on June 15: "Holden Roberto arrived in Mogadiscio in order to take part in top-level OAU talks accompanying President Mobutu Sese Seko of Zaire with whom he recently visited Peking.

"In an interview Holden Roberto declared that now his enemies could not accuse him of being an anti-socialist because FNLA soldiers were now being trained by Chinese instructors."

So Roberto was beginning to pose as a socialist, but his argument in support of this was much too feeble. The leader of the Chilean junta Pinochet, for example, could have also said that he was not an anti-communist simply because he was on the best of terms with Peking which furnished him selfless aid and support. Of course, a declaration of this sort merely showed that CIA agent Guilmore-Roberto had a shallow mind; at the same time however it made one stop and think: for what purpose the Chinese instructors trained the armed bands that were being assembled in a number of military camps placed by Zaire's ruling circles at the disposal of Holden Roberto and his henchmen?

Roberto claimed that the men who were herded into military camps were "volunteers".

In the wake of the instructors from China large consignments of Chinese arms and ammunition began to arrive in Zaire. On September 11 the Lisbon newspaper *O Seculo* carried a Reuter's report from Kinshasa dated the previous day, which said: "Today the FNLA announced that it has received 450 tons of military equipment as a gift from China. The

FNLA communique circulated by the Zaire News Agency (AZAP) states that China has also sent a large quantity of materials to be used in the FNLA-controlled zones in Angola."

It will be recalled that in the early days of September there were no FNLA-controlled zones in Angola, for, as I have mentioned in the previous chapter, Roberto's detachments entered Angola's northern provinces at the end of September.

According to specialists, at the end of September he had only two or three thousand men under his command. But by the end of 1974 Chinese instructors had trained and equipped enough men in the territory of Zaire to form a whole division.

Besides supporting Holden Roberto, the Chinese did not forget the second organisation, the UNITA. As we know Jonas Savimbi was to have been included in the puppet government which reactionary circles among the white settlers intended to set up after executing a rightist coup in Angola simultaneously with a revolt that was to take place in Portugal in September 1974. The plan was foiled. Some of the conspirators were arrested and the rest fled, most of them to South Africa. Nevertheless, in its daily reports from Angola the world press continued to mention Jonas Savimbi and his UNITA, and the plan to use his organisation as the second striking force against the MPLA was conceived precisely in that period. But the three hundred men who comprised the organisation's "military units" at the end of 1974 were a negligible threat to the well-trained MPLA army with its long years' experience in guerrilla warfare. There was only Jonas Savimbi and a handful of his henchmen—a general without an army. Therefore it was necessary to raise an army, or at least a semblance of one for the "general". And here, once again, Peking decided to help. On March 17, 1975 a France Press correspondent reported from Lusaka that on that day a UNITA delegation led by the organisation's general secretary Samuel Chiwala left the city for Peking and was seen off at the airport by officials of the Chinese Embassy.

Chiwala was not a newcomer to Peking. He first visited the city years earlier when he and Jonas Savimbi were sent there by Holden Roberto. Then they were two unknown men, whereas now Chiwala was a distinguished guest. On March 21 two black limousines drove into a side street near the western part of the Avenue of Great Tranquility in Chang An-tse district near the city's centre and pulled up at the gate of a respectable looking Chinese-style building. It was the Chinese People's Association for Friendship with the Peoples of Foreign Countries. Awaiting the guests in the reception chamber were Association Chairman Chai Tse-min, his deputy Yang Chi and two interpreters. The door opened and a group of Africans led by Samuel Chiwala entered.

At first the hosts asked their guests about their trip, their health, the health of their relatives and about the health of UNITA President Jonas Savimbi and his relatives. That lasted for a few minutes. Then Chai Tse-min poured tea into small bowls, moved a box of Chinese cigarettes closer to the guests, indicating that it was time to turn to business. Chiwala extracted a few sheets of paper from a black folder and began to read out UNITA's needs and requirements which the Chinese would have to satisfy if they expected the organisation actively to operate against the MPLA and effectively support Roberto's forces in the north of the country.

The meeting took place, to use a clishé, in a friendly and cordial atmosphere and both sides displayed mutual understanding. The UNITA delegation's visit lasted for almost a month. On March 31 the Hsinhua Agency reported from Peking: "Today Vice Premier of the PRC State Council Teng Hsiao-ping had a meeting with General Secretary of the UNITA S. Chiwala and the UNITA delegation which he heads. The two sides had a friendly and cordial conversation.

"Present at the meeting were Chairman of the Chinese People's Association for Friendship with the Peoples of Foreign Countries Chai Tse-min, his Deputy Yang Chi and others."

Commenting on Peking's machinations, the Senegalese newspaper Le Soleil wrote at the time that the PRC assisted those forces in Angola which did not have the backing of the Angolan people.

The Chinese leaders did not confine themselves to supporting the reaction in Angola alone, hoping that it would gain the upper hand over the MPLA. Peking had far greater designs and planned to play a major role in bringing about division among the African countries. Believing that right-wing forces in the African continent had better chances for success, the Chinese began strengthening their links with South African racialists. It should be noted that China was already receiving South African cotton, wool, copper, gold, and diamonds and had signed an agreement with the Republic of South Africa to deliver it Chinese oil, and was also importing chromium and graphite from Rhodesia. Some of the commercial operations with these countries were conducted through Japan and the Portuguese colony of Macao. Peking's dual diplomacy could not remain a secret for long if only because the Chinese themselves were not too anxious to hide such contacts from the rest of the world.

On October 10, 1975, for example, the South African *Rand Daily Mail* carried a report from Singapore which said that the abrupt and amazing shift in Peking's policy towards Pretoria in the previous month came as a complete surprise for some South Africans, when they learned that in his speech at a banquet in honour of a distinguished guest from Zambia Deputy Premier of the PRC State Council Li Hsien-nien hinted that China approved the dialogue started by African states with the Republic of South Africa and Rhodesia.

It was also evident to the Peking policy-makers that their flirtation with South African racialists would not affect their relations with Jonas Savimbi and Holden Roberto who were also maintaining close contacts with Pretoria. For example Jonas Savimbi told a correspondent of the Johannesburg weekly *Southern African Financial Mail* in May 1975 that he trusted Vorster who said that South Africa would establish economic cooperation with Angola after the latter becomes independent. He said he hoped that Angola's future leaders would cooperate with the Republic of South Africa. Pointing to the construction of a dam on the Cunene as an example of such cooperation, he noted that it was not the only one. Asked whether he thought that South Africa should be ostracised, Savimbi replied that he did not believe that it should, adding that he expected her leaders to be realistic and consent to establishing political and economic cooperation with other countries in spite of the differences in their political systems. The Republic of South Africa, he said, was an independent state and the abolition of apartheid was a separate issue. He emphasised that it was impossible to secure the development of Angola without support and assistance by private enterprises, including foreign companies, and that the latter should not be nationalised in Angola. Nationalisation, Savimbi said, was a malady.

Such were the plans harboured by a leader of one of the groups which Peking supported.

Peking's full and unequivocal support for the imperialist policy of the US ruling circles, and their search for contacts with the South African racialists and approval of their foreign policy did not immediately meet with a rebuff on the African continent. There were states which at first simply refused to believe that such treachery was possible. On July 14, 1975 the *Afrique-Asie* journal published an interesting confession by an African leader following his visit to Peking. Until recently, the journal wrote, China's stand was unclear, but then the head of an African state informed us of his own official demarches to Peking undertaken with the view to making China terminate her support for the FNLA. I made it clear to the Chinese premier, he told us, that we could not understand how people's China could give any sort of assistance to an organisation which had been raised, financed and operated by the CIA, and whose real aim was to suppress the independence of the Angolan people. The explanation which was given to me, the head of the African state said, was unsatisfactory and I said so frankly as befitting a true revolutionary.... Is it possible to view the Chinese Government's decision to aid such vile traitors of their people as Roberto and Savimbi as anything else than a carefully considered political step?

But while African functionaries doubted China's true intentions, the western bourgeois press found them in the order of things and considered Peking's actions as a logical continuation of its anti-communist, pro-imperialist line. Reports from Angola in those days were replete with phrases such as: ".... The North, controlled by the anti-Soviet, but pro-Chinese National Front for the Liberation of Angola (FNLA)..." (taken from a report filed by a France Press correspondent in Luanda on July 19, 1975).

By July 1975 MPLA forces controlled twelve out of the country's sixteen provinces and were in full control in the capital of Angola, Luanda. Roberto's and Savimbi's bands were on the brink of utter defeat. In these circumstances their benefactors decided to increase the shipments of arms and ammunition to them, accelerate their military training and grant them bigger financial assistance.

One day at the end of July a car with a US flag drove up to the Foreign Ministry in Peking as the head of the US Mission in the PRC George Herbert Walker Bush arrived to pay a regular visit to Deputy Foreign Minister Ho Ying. Still it was not a routine call, but a strictly confidential meeting at which the Angolan issue was discussed. The Chinese side also included the head of African Department of the Foreign Ministry Ho Kung-kai and his deputy Chou Ming-chi. Information about what had transpired at this meeting reached the African continent about a month later. In August, the Sierra-Leone newspaper *Nation* wrote that Chinese and US officials met several times in Peking to exchange views on the situation in Angola, on measures which should be taken to help the FNLA. They agreed among other things that China would increase arms deliveries to Angola and that Chinese military advisers and instructors should be with the FNLA forces in the field.

Other sources reported that, besides China's Deputy Foreign Minister Ho Ying, some of the meetings at which Angola was discussed were also attended by Deputy Foreign Minister Wang Hai Jung.

At their talks in Peking the US and Chinese sides agreed that the US Military Mission in Kinshasa would coordinate its activity with the Chinese advisers attached to Holden Roberto's bands. In this connection an interesting item was published in *Diario de Luanda* on October 21, 1975, in which the FNLA was characterised as a multinational establishment.

A commentary published by *Do Journal do Brazil* in its column "J. B. Informs" began with the words: "The military situation in Angola has produced the most fantastic multinational establishment imaginable." Dwelling on Holden Roberto's FNLA "army", the commentary went on to say ". . . The FNLA's chief strategist is a Portuguese colonel who had served in Salazar's army. Above him stands a General Staff which employs two Chinese generals who appear in the streets of Kinshasa in Zaire wearing their Peking military uniforms. These generals guide the US military mission consisting of 15 officers who also openly appear in the streets in their military uniforms." Indeed it was a multinational cohort determined at whatever the cost to bring Holden Roberto and his clique to power in Angola.

In the second half of 1975 China sharply increased deliveries of military supplies to the UNITA and the FNLA, which also began to receive Peking's financial aid which grew in size from month to month. It is interesting to note that Chinese subsidies reached the UNITA through London where the organisation was represented by a South African clergyman I. Busch.

The so-called foreign minister of the FNLA-UNITA coalition Wahall Neto circulated a statement in Kinshasa on December 14 highly praising the PRC and calling China "a reliable comrade in arms of the UNITA-FNLA coalition in the struggle". In the struggle against whom? In the struggle against the MPLA, the sole legitimate representative of the Angolan people, against the People's Republic of Angola which by then had already been recognised by many countries.

October and November 1975 were perhaps the most difficult months in Angola's history. The Angolans fought against foreign intervention. The enemy was driving on the capital and Roberto's bands supported by mercenaries were deployed just 22 kilometres north of it. This was in the middle of October and the *Pravda* sent me on my third assignment to Angola for on the spot information about the situation there. Here are passages from my travel diary covering those days.

October 28

Hotel Tivoli in Luanda where almost all foreign journalists who had come to cover the events in Angola were booked resembled a human anthill. From early morning until late at night the lobby was packed with representatives of the press, radio and television. They exchanged news, queued up at night for a turn at the only available telex set, lost their tempers when communication proved difficult and tried to analyse the situation in their reports and commentaries. In those days, two weeks prior to the proclamation of independence, the situation in the country, particularly in the capital, Luanda, was very complicated and difficult. Difficult for the Angolan people and their vanguard the MPLA under whose guidance the population for more than 14 years waged an armed struggle for freedom and independence.

I arrived in Luanda on October 25. Two days earlier MPLA army detachments had halted the enemy about 25 kilometres from the capital's northern boundary, approximately at Kifangondo, a small locality with a water tower and a pumping station which supplied Luanda with fresh water.

On the central front enemy units had concentrated in the area of Nova Lisboa, Angola's second biggest city, and were making desperate attempts to break through to Mocamedes, Benguela and Lobito, the country's main ports.

Enemy motorised columns were moving from the Namibian border in the south in an effort to link up with the units standing at Nova Lisboa, and then launch an offensive on Luanda from the south with the principal objective of capturing a place called Donda with a power station that supplied Luanda with electricity. Such was the situation, in purely military terms, on October 25, 1975.

Yesterday, October 27, Comrade Paulette of the Information Ministry's press sector told me: "Tomorrow the MPLA leadership intends to take a group of journalists to one of the northern sectors of the front. If you wish we'll include you and the Pole Ryszard Kapuściński into it." Naturally Ryszard and I were tremendously pleased at the prospect of visiting MPLA army units stationed on one of Angola's main fronts, the Northern Front, on whose western flank the enemy positions were only 25 kilometres from Luanda. But since we were assured that the entire trip would take only 12 hours, all of us thought that we would be taken to the nearest sector and decided to bring only our cameras and film along.

On the following day, however, our escort announced that we will be taken to Salazar, a town situated 250 kilometres east of Luanda, and would return only on the next day.

We left Luanda at daybreak planning to reach a place called Kuso by midday, where as we were informed MPLA units were preparing for an offensive against enemy detachments consisting of FNLA troops and mercenaries.

The last checkpoint was some 15 kilometres north of the small town of Lukala. Two soldiers with submachine guns stopped our bus, examined the permit issued by the MPLA Army HQ and the Information Ministry, counted the passengers, saluted and wished us luck. The driver got the bus moving and we headed for Kuso, our destination.

Kuso is not to be found on an ordinary map. To get an idea where this section of the front passed it is necessary to mark off a sector 250 kilometres east of Luanda. There you will find Kuso, standing on a highway leading to the coffee province of Uige. This region, including Salazar (now called Ndalatandu) had been occupied by the enemy for a long time and was recaptured by the MPLA only about a month ago.

It was a rolling country and the gentle slopes of the hills were covered with thousands of coffee trees, coconut palm groves and sisal and cotton plantations. But in their overwhelming majority the fields were overgrown with grasses and weeds. A dead, abandoned land. The local population had fled to larger villages and towns from the FNLA bands and the wild brutalities of the mercenaries. Formerly one of the most flourishing parts of northern Angola, this area was now empty and devastated.

In the centre of Ndalatandu stands an old colonial-type Portuguese fortress. An MPLA unit was billeted there. Discovering that we were journalists its commander offered to show us the weapons which were captured from the enemy in the latest operation. The MPLA fighters brought out and heaped right on the pavement dozens of US, French and Belgian submachine guns, mortars, anti-tank rifles, shells and boxes with ammunition and also weapons and ammunition marked with Chinese characters—Peking's deliveries to the imperialist hirelings.

Former Portuguese Army Captain Artur Queiroz, journalist of *Diario de Luanda*, was particularly interested in the Chinese weapons which made up the bigger portion of the heap. His face grew darker and darker and he kept shrugging his shoulders and shaking his head in surprise. Then, turning to Ryszard and me he said: "You know, I've been under the influence of Peking propaganda for the past two or three years. It seemed to me that there was something revolutionary in it which was worthy of studying and implementing in Angola. Gradually, however, I began to doubt that my views were correct, and what I've learned lately has finally opened my eyes. Is it possible to call people, who supply weapons to the deadly enemies of my people, who slander the MPLA and act hand in hand with NATO, revolutionaries supporting the national liberation struggle. When I get back to my newspaper I'll definitely write a long article about the Peking opportunists."

Nineteen kilometres from Lukala we stopped at what had once been a village, almost directly on the highway. The skeletons of walls formed two even rows on the scorched land. Here and there we saw charred posts with twisted basins and pots, and fragments of pitchers and crushed gourds in which Angolan peasants usually keep fresh water scattered all around them. The wrecked walls resembled some strange tombstones. Stepping over heaps of cold embers and ashes we entered a gutted hut. We got the impression that the interventionists moved from hut to hut igniting the straw roofs from the inside. There were no signs of a battle and the line of the front did not pass through the village. We made a thorough scrutiny and failed to discover even one bullet hole. Learning that the interventionists were approaching, the peasants fled for safety to the southern regions which were controlled by the MPLA forces. But the enemy carried on his dirty work of pillaging, burning and destroying.

On our way we saw other gutted villages and each one presented an identical picture of the enemy's vandalism. But the sight which still awaited us on that day dwarfed all other scenes of devastation.

Close to the road we spotted an intact building standing in a circle of charred posts. The words Fazenda Lico were painted in white on its tiled roof. Evidently it had once belonged to a white settler. Just here the road made a sharp bend and the driver slowed down. Suddenly he jammed on the brakes, stopped the bus and shouted: "Look, look." On either side of the road ahead of us lay the bodies of women, children and old people. All of them were dead, shot down by machine gun fire. This horrible scene of senseless slaughter shocked us to such an extent that we had not the heart to count the corpses. And scattered all around them, on the shrubs and the wilted grass were old clothes, shoes and other belongings which the marauders and killers from the interventionist bands left behind after ripping open the bundles into which they had been tied.

Back in Lukala we had picked up an old peasant who asked for a lift to Fazenda Lico. Now the driver opened the door and the old man got off. He took a few steps in the direction of the corpses and then sank to the ground, his hands clasping his head. We raised him to his feet and seated him on a stone near the road. Rocking from side to side he kept on talking in the local dialect. Our group included a staff member of the national radio station in Luanda and I asked him to interpret. It turned out that the peasant was the only one of these refugees who had survived an attack by the FNLA band and mercenaries.

. . .It happened several days ago when enemy forces took over the town of Samba-Kasu. All the townsfolk had fled, and as they passed through these places advised the peasants to go away as quickly as possible. And so when the sounds of exploding mines and shells in the north became clearly audible in the village, all the peasants decided to leave their homes and seek shelter either in Lukala or Ndalatandu. Tying their belongings into bundles they headed in a single file in a southerly direction. The commander of an MPLA platoon which was stationed in the village ordered four young fighters, each about 16 years of age armed with rifles to escort the peasants and protect them if they should be intercepted by bandits.

But neither the platoon commander nor the peasants knew that, while they were getting ready for the journey, about 30 FNLA bandits managed to slip past MPLA outposts, penetrated into the rear of the MPLA army and laid an ambush in the vicinity of the abandoned Fazenda Lico.

After a while the peasants, particularly the children grew tired of walking in the scorching sun, and the babies wanted to eat. And so the MPLA fighters decided to make a stop at Lico, cook some food, feed the kids, rest and then continue the trek to Lukala. But before they reached the fazenda the peasants were swept by machine-gun fire from the nearby bushes. Several women fell to the ground, blood streaming from their wounds. The children screamed. Then armed men jumped onto the road from either side firing at point blank range at the peasants. About ten of them rushed the MPLA boys who did not even have a chance of firing a single shot. The FNLA men trampled on the corpses emptying their guns at those who still showed signs of life. The old man who told us this had a miraculous escape. He rolled into a ditch and a dead woman with a bullet-riddled child in her arms fell on top of him.

The next act of this massacre was no less blood-curdling. First the FNLA cutthroats tied the hands of the captured MPLA fighters behind their backs. Then they brought a can of petrol from an abandoned lorry standing near the estate, poured the liguid over the unfortunates, ignited it and let them loose. Mad with pain the four human torches rushed about the field and rolled on the ground trying to extinguish the flames. Finally, they collapsed never to rise again. One of them dropped some two paces from the old man who was hiding in the ditch and he saw how the flames licked the boy's face.

One can hear innumerable accounts of atrocities committed by the interventionists and their puppets in any district in Luanda where there is a concentration of refugees who have fled to the capital from various regions of the country temporarily occupied by the FNLA and UNITA bands, mercenaries from different countries, butchers from the detachments of former agents of the Portuguese secret police (PIDE) and fascists from the so-called Portuguese Liberation Army. I have mentioned only one fact which I and the other journalists who made the trip to Lukala can confirm documentarily. The charred bodies of the MPLA fighters, the corpses of the shot women and children summon all honest people to come out against such savagery.

According to a report which appeared recently in the US press, there is a bureau in Fresno, California, for recruiting all those who had taken part in similar operations during the US aggression in Vietnam and now wanted to go to Angola. About 400 such cutthroats were already waiting to be dispatched to Africa and turn it into a scene of dozens of Mai Lais. The scum of the earth—South African racialists, former members of the Portuguese secret police and servicemen who had taken part in US punitive operations in Vietnam—will stop at nothing in order to throttle the young republic.

October 30

Two landrovers drove up at five in the morning. A submachine gunner who knew local dialects and also spoke Portuguese and could act as interpreter was attached to Ryszard and myself. He was a very nice lad of about 17 and tried to be helpful. He volunteered to carry our cameras and was greatly disappointed when we said that it was as much our duty to carry them ourselves as it was his duty to carry his submachine gun.

We entered Samba-Kazu with the first MPLA detachments. The men piled the captured submachine guns, mortars, bazookas and hand grenades, most of which were made in China, into a lorry. I made several photographs of a Chinese made antiaircraft machine gun. Fighting was still going on on the outskirts and we could hear the explosions of mines and bursts of submachine-gun fire.

The order to return came when the sun was already high over the horizon, just as we were asking the MPLA unit commander about the results of the operation so that back in Luanda we would be able to send first-hand news to our editorial offices without having to wait for an official communique.

"We've lost only four men," he said.

"Five," said the commissar who was also present. "I've just heard that a Chinese mortar shell scored a direct hit on Justinho Samedo." Turning towards us he added: "You knew him. He was your interpreter."

We were back in Luanda at 20.00 hours. By then I had already taped a communique about the situation at the fronts which also contained a report about the capture of Samba-Kazu. As Igor Uvarov of TASS and I compiled the information we intended to communicate to the *Pravda* the following morning by telex, I included into the part of the communique which mentioned the capture of Samba-Kazu the following lines: "This correspondent witnessed the operation and entered the town with the advance MPLA detachment.... Upon inspecting the trophies we were struck by the large amount of Chinese weapons and ammunition." I also wanted to write about Justinho Samedo who was killed by Chinese-made mortar shells, but refrained from doing so because many other people in other sectors of the front were being killed by shells, bullets and mines which the Chinese were delivering to Roberto's and Savimbi's bands.

Who trained the FNLA and UNITA bands, who taught them to plunder, rape, and torture the local population? "All my soldiers are trained by the Chinese," said Holden Roberto, the FNLA chief, in an interview with *Le Monde* on June 6, 1975. "I'm a great admirer of the Chinese and everything they have achieved because the Chinese gave me unconditional aid," he stressed.

In a statement in Lusaka on January 25, 1976 Jonas Savimbi said: "We have specialists who were trained in China and who are evolving guerrilla tactics for us."

Bandits trained by the Chinese instructors, bandits armed by Peking. After the arrival of the first consignment of 450 tons of weapons for the FNLA in the middle of 1974, military supplies from China poured in a steady stream. A Reuter's correspondent in Luanda told Uvarov and me on October 31, 1975 that he sent a report to his agency about the FNLA army saying that it numbered 25,000 men and was equipped with Chinese semi-automatic rifles, hand grenades, mortars, recoilless guns, rocket launchers and armoured personnel carriers. Later we learned from Portuguese sources that the bulk of this equipment was brought to Angola overland from the northern border towns of Banza Sosso and Buela, about

210 kilometres from the Zairean capital Kinshasa and also by sea from the Zairean port of Matadi to the ports of Santo Antonio do Zaire and Ambrizete in Northwestern Angola.

On July 7, 1975 *The Washington Post* carried the following report sent in by its correspondent David B. Ottaway: "Chinese arms and supplies for the National Front (FNLA—*Ed.*) come into Angola across the largely unguarded Zaire border and are then brought south by road through front-controlled territory.... The Chinese also gave some arms initially to the third guerrilla group, the National Union for the Total Idependence of Angola (UNITA—Ed.)...."

Ottaway deliberately used the word "initially" in reference to deliveries of Chinese weapons to the UNITA in order to hint that subsequently Peking withdrew its support for this organisation. Calculated to mislead public opinion, this was yet another attempt to move the UNITA into the forefront as an organisation which "no side" supports and which, consequently, could speak on behalf of the whole of Angola.

Claims of this sort were refuted by statements issued by the UNITA itself. One of them disclosed that China had agreed to send a large consignment of weapons to the UNITA which it badly needed. This admission was published in the Zambian capital on December 31, 1975, and meant that even when the FNLA and UNITA bands began to suffer heavy defeats at the hands of the patriots, Peking still hoped to remedy the situation and continued to supply them with arms.

The general tenor of the reports carried by the Western press gave a clear indication of the plans which were being hatched by the coalition of ultra-reactionary forces at a time when it became obvious that the FNLA and UNITA were losing the battle for Angola.

Here is an excerpt from an article by Leslie Gelb published by *The New York Times* at September of 1975: "All odds now favoured victory of the ... Popular Movement in Angola, unless the United States and China rushed huge transfusions of aid...."

The following extract is from a report by Colin Legum in the London *Observer* of January 18, 1976: "...For the Vorster Regime, the victory of ... MPLA would be a bitter blow but without major Western or Chinese intervention the South Africans' present involvement appears untenable."

Until the very last Peking leaders hoped that fortune would turn and help their wards. On the eve of Roberto's final rout, when the press reported that his links with Peking were weakening, the FNLA chief gave an interview to Michael Salomon of the South African *Rand Daily Mail* which was published on February 5, 1976. When Salomon said that there was a lot of talk of a "split between China and yourself", Roberto laughed and replied that he was seeing the Chinese ambassador of the People's Republic in Kinshasa regularly, as well as receiving friendly delegations from Peking, and there was no sign of a split.

In the same interview Roberto said: "We had a contract with the Chinese Government for military experts until August 1975. This was extended until November 11...." And added that at present he had a liaison mission which maintained contacts with Peking.

Concluding my account of Peking's activity in Angola, I would like to quote some assessments of Peking's policy which were published in various parts of the world.

Western Hemisphere

A quotation from the Spanish issue of *Newsweek* magazine of December 22, 1975: "The inflexibly anti-communist government of South Africa appears to be interested in establishing diplomatic relations with communist China. Recently a South African scholar who is adviser to Prime Minister John Vorster publicly declared that such a link was necessary.... South Africa and China support one and the same side in the civil war in Angola, while the Russians are on the other side.

"Although it seems improbable that the Chinese want to impair their image in the eyes of the Third World countries by sharing a common stand with the racialist South Africa, Peking, nevertheless, could have resorted to hidden forms of cooperation."

Early in February 1976 the Peruvian weekly *Estampa* wrote as follows:

"The Peking leaders have completely deviated from the principles of international socialist and proletarian solidarity. They are in the camp of those who are engaged in aggression against one of the biggest national liberation movements in recent years—the MPLA.

"The just cause of the Angolan patriots is getting the upper hand in the country, and together with them—the revolutionary forces of the world."

In a report on March 14, 1976 the Cuban newspaper *Granma* observed: "It was precisely the racialists, the mercenaries and the bands of Jonas Savimbi and Holden Roberto equipped with Chinese weapons and trained by Chinese military advisers who destroyed, plundered, tortured and burned Angolan patriots. It was they who killed thousands of Angolans prior to taking to their heels in the north, east and south. It was they who killed women, old people and children, taking their revenge on the inhabitants of the regions which rejected them."

Asia

"In the opinion of some Western observers," wrote the *Hindustan Times* on February 3, 1976, "the Angolan war has been an 'unmitigated disaster' to Chinese foreign policy the core of which is confrontation with the Soviet Union wherever and whenever possible. In fact so far-reaching have been the repercussions of Angola that they affect Chinese diplomacy far beyond Africa. . . ."

Europe

The *Quotidien de Paris* on February 25, 1976 carried an item which said in part: "The war in Vietnam was barely over when China with the America of Kissinger and the CIA began activating the war in Angola and came running to the aid of the FNLA. . . . In this way China tried its best to create a new and salvational 'seat of distraction' for Soviet 'social-imperialism' at the expense of the United States. But China played the wrong horse."

Another French paper, *France-Soir* on January 15: ". . .Strange as it may seem the Americans, the Chinese and the very discreet French mission found themselves side by side supporting the rebels in the north. . ."

On December 12, 1975 the Swedish *Arbetartidningen Ny Dag* carried an editorial entitled "Self-isolation" which contained the following observation: "China pursues a pro-imperialist policy. Peking's sole guiding principle in this policy is that of always occupying a stand opposite to that of the Soviet Union. This is accompanied by accusations and outright slander levelled against the Soviet Union.... China's stand towards Angola is a striking example of Chinese foreign policy which places itself in opposition virtually to every liberation movement, every resistance movement fighting against fascist oppression.

"Chinese foreign policy is pursued under the motto: 'unite many, isolate a few'. In practice, however, this objective is achieved not in the way Peking leaders would have liked. Peking is on the way to isolating itself from the world-wide anti-imperialist movement."

Airica

The Senegalese journal *L'Observateur Africain* published in Dakar made the following comment in February 1976: "Peking's role is particularly despicable. Providing financial and military aid to Roberto's and Savimbi's cutthroats, China maliciously attacks the MPLA, the People's Republic of Angola and the states which support them, the Soviet Union in the first place.... Peking leaders have in fact formed an alliance not only with the CIA but also with the South African racialists."

The African Communist, the official organ of the South African Communist Party, had this to say in its February issue:".... It is sad to have to note once again that China's wrong foreign policy has landed her in the imperialist camp. To the long list of disastrous adventures—Indonesia, the Sudan, Chile, Bangladesh etc.—must now be added the shameful history of Chinese backing of the forces oposed to MPLA.

"These are not accidents or aberrations, but flow from the central theme of Chinese foreign policy.... China ... is ... prepared to enter into alliances with the imperialists in order to mobilise the maximum possible force against the Soviet Union and its allies. Pursuing this line, China has even come out in support of Vorster's policy of 'detente' and 'dialogue' with Africa."

Here is an extract from a report carried by *Agencia Angola Press* at the end of August 1975. "By pursuing a policy which clashes with the interests of the Angolan masses, China does not simply support the most reactionary forces in Angola thus siding with the imperialist forces, but actively supplies the FNLA with fairly large consignments of light and heavy weapons."

On December 23, 1975 in an article dealing on the splitting activity of Peking the *Jornal de Angola* wrote that while speaking up in defence of the small nations Peking in fact strives to dictate to them and undermines their struggle for real national liberation. By supporting the reactionaries and the enemies of the Angolan people, the newspaper wrote, the Chinese leaders once again expose themselves to the whole world as undisguised champions of imperialism.

So, during the events in Angola Peking again showed the world that it acts as the abettor and an ally of the world's most ominous forces.

Chapter VI

South African Racialists Move into Angola

After fascism had been overthrown in Portugal and it became clear that her new, revolutionary authorities were determined to end the colonial war and begin talks on the question of recognising the national liberation movements as the sole legitimate representatives of the peoples of their respective countries, the pro-imperialist forces immediately decided to coordinate their actions in the hope of forming a united front and working out a common programme of action.

With this aim in view Provisional President of Portugal General Spínola met US President Nixon. The meeting took place in the afternoon of June 19, 1974 in the Azores in Officers' Club No. 4 at the Lajes air base near Angra do Heroismo, and lasted more than 90 minutes.

It was described as a "working meeting" at which the future of the Portuguese colonies in Africa, particularly Angola where the US had considerable capital investments, was discussed.

At about the same time Chief of the General Staff of the Republic of South Africa Admiral Hugo Bierman made a "private visit" to the United States where he conferred with Chairman of the Joint Chiefs of Staff Admiral Thomas N. Moorer and other top US officials. Commenting on the trip *The Christian Science Monitor* wrote that the South Africans dreamt of US cooperation in preventing the threat, which was originating in Mozambique and Angola, from spreading to Rhodesia and South Africa.

As you already know on September 14 General Spínola made another trip, this time to the Island of Sal where he had talks with President Mobutu of Zaire who was accompanied by Holden Roberto.

I have mentioned three fairly high-level meetings which became known to world public opinion. But there were many other meetings involving officials of a lower rank which were not reported by the mass media. And so a sort of a quadripartite arrangement took shape in the latter half of 1974 involving Portugal (General Spínola and his associates), the United States (Pentagon and the CIA), South Africa and Zaire. After the events of September 1974, when General Spínola was forced to resign from the post of provisional president and dropped out of the picture, it became a tripartite arrangement between the USA, South Africa and Zaire.

Initially Zaire alone was in a position to undertake direct action and she moved Holden Roberto's bands into Angola's northern provinces. But the three conspirators maintained close contacts and coordinated their plans which were implemented by UNITA and the FNLA plus ultra Right-wing organisations made up of white settlers, former PIDE agents, the "Portuguese Liberation Army" and Right-wing parties. In July there were racial clashes in Luanda which carried away about 500 lives. They were provoked by reactionary circles among the white settlers who had devised a programme for preventing the decolonisation of Angola. The racialist organisation Union of Resistance of Angola (RUA) which was linked with South Africa posted leaflets in the city demanding the proclamation of Angolan "independence" patterned along Rhodesian lines.

Within a few months following the overthrow of fascism in Portugal UNITA leaders warned SWAPO (South West Africa People's Organization, fighting for the liberation of Namibia) not to undertake military operations against South African troops. Already at that time those SWAPO members whom the UNITA had disarmed and confined to camps in Nova Lisboa told visiting correspondents that the UNITA had connived with the South African Army. Wilson, one of UNITA leaders, clearly expounded his organisation's stand when he admitted in the middle of November in Luanda that if it came to power in independent Angola it would not aid any liberation movement in Southwest Africa. We want good relations with all our neighbours, he said. They have problems which they have to solve on their own and Namibia, too, must decide her own future.

At the end of 1974 UNITA chief Jonas Savimbi visited

several African countries. In this connection the Swiss *Neue Zürcher Zeitung* observed: "UNITA leader Jonas Savimbi is visiting Gabon and Ivory Coast. It can be presumed that Savimbi's UNITA is playing an important role in South Africa's activities towards Black Africa. In these activities Abidjan and Liberville occupy a prominent place."

Following the formation of a provisional government in Angola Jonas Savimbi became more outspoken and did not conceal that he intended to establish the closest links with the racialist regime in South Africa in the future. At the end of January 1975 he made a statement in the Zambian capital in which he outlined steps for strengthening relations with South Africa. Commenting on this statement *The Times of Zambia* wrote on February 5 that UNITA leader Dr. Jonas Savimbi had recently declared in Lusaka that the Provisional Government of Angola would revise economic and other agreements between the colonial government of Angola and the Government of South Africa in the light of political but not economic aspects.

Continuing the paper quoted Savimbi as saying that the revision of economic assistance on the part of South Africa would depend on the attitude of the South Africans themselves, but in his opinion it was necessary to talk with the South Africans and only then decide what to do.

The paper went on to say that Savimbi who believed South Africa would take part in the economic development of Angola had a great deal of work in store for him. South Africans were the shareholders or direct or indirect owners of the Benguela Railway, oil companies, diamond mines, the banking system and had major investments in Angola.

Savimbi repeatedly referred to relations with South Africa in statements which he made in the next few months. On May 1, 1975 the *Afrique-Asie* journal summed up his views as follows: "Economic cooperation with South Africa is a reality.... The armed liberation struggle will not resolve the problem of Namibia, South Africa and Rhodesia.... It is necessary to develop the policy of dialogue and clarification. Savimbi said so on April 29 in Luanda and asserted that the South African Prime Minister was a responsible person.... For some months already the South African press is eulogising the UNITA and its leader. The official organ of South Africa *Die Burger* had devoted many pages to Savimbi...."

On its part the FNLA was also establishing very close contacts with the Republic of South Africa. Early in July 1975 one of its leaders Daniel Chipenda went to Namibia which was occupied by South Africa, where he met the head of the South African State Security Bureau General Van den Berg in Windhoek. Their talks went on for three days. Two months later Chipenda once again flew to the south of the African continent, this time to South Africa, where he signed an agreement with the Vorster Government on South African financial and military assistance to the FNLA.

Later, in February 1976, Defence Minister of the People's Republic of Angola Henrique Teles Carriera in an interview with the Italian newspaper *Republica* would describe the situation in the country at that time in the following terms: "We arrived at the conclusion that already prior to our independence Zaire and South Africa had worked out a joint political and military plan not without the participation of the United States. And when in the middle of last year it became clear that the MPLA would soon strengthen its control over the whole country, the leaders of Kinshasa and Pretoria decided to resort to military operations in order to install a purely neocolonialist type of government consisting of FNLA and UNITA representatives in Luanda prior to November 11."

August 8, 1975 can be regarded as the beginning of direct South African aggression against Angola. On that day regular South African troops crossed the border into the south of Angola allegedly to assume control over the large Calueque dam on the Cunene. The hydropower scheme on the river includes a pumping station which supplies water to Ovamboland in the north of Namibia. Calueque is a part of the Cunene scheme whose construction was launched in 1969 by the Portuguese colonial authorities and the South African government. Another dam, the Ruakana, likewise on the Cunene, is situated close to the Namibian border and with the Calueque pumping station forms the nucleus of the entire scheme.

On August 12 the Portuguese governor of Cunene Region went to Lisbon in connection with developments on the territory under his control.

On August 22, two weeks after the first incursion, fresh contingents of South African troops invaded Angola from

Namibia, crossed the border at Santa Clara and captured the town of Namakundo.

By August 26 they had advanced towards the town of Chiede and came up to the capital of the Cunene province Pereira d'Eça.

In view of the events in the south of Angola the MPLA issued a communique which said that essentially there was no difference between the arrival of South African troops in the southern part of Angola from what had taken place in Uiga and Zaire, Angola's northern provinces bordering on the Republic of Zaire. The communique also vigorously protested to the South African authorities "about this encroachment and aggression" and demanded the immediate withdrawal of its troops from Angolan territory.

It is important to note that immediately after South Africa had launched an armed aggression against Angola, the Command of the South African troops established contact and interaction with the UNITA. When Jonas Savimbi was in Senegal at the end of October he gave an interview to *Le Soleil* newspaper in which he acknowledged that military and political control in the Cunene region whose southern part was occupied by South African troops was exercised by UNITA Foreign Affairs Secretary A. Vakulukuta. And displaying touching reciprocity the FNLA and UNITA manifested their gratitude to the South African aggressors by graciously granting command posts in areas temporarily occupied by their bands to South African representatives. For example, South African General Muller was "governor" of Sá da Bandeira which was under their control in November and December 1975.

After capturing the Cunene province the South African troops for a while refrained from advancing deeper into Angola in the hope that the FNLA and UNITA would manage to defeat the MPLA. But this did not mean that South Africa chose to be a bystander temporarily staying on foreign territory. The direct invasion of the Cunene province by the South African imperialists coincided with the beginning of an airlift of arms and weapons for UNITA and FNLA bands from South Africa to Silva Porto and Negage.

At about the same time South African instructors began arriving in Silva Porto, a UNITA base, and in Negage, the FNLA's main base. Philippe Essomba, a correspondent of the French weekly *Jeune Afrique*, filed the following report after visiting the UNITA base in Silva Porto. "In Silva Porto we saw five white soldiers driving the Panhard armoured personnel carriers. Replying to our questions they said that they were of British nationality. But a five minutes' conversation made it absolutely clear to my British colleagues that they spoke with a typical South African accent. There were similar scenes in Benguela and Lobito, two towns which the UNITA and the FNLA had captured from the MPLA. When the journalists arrived fifty young white soldiers hastily hid themselves behind large lorries. They, too, were South Africans. UNITA leader Jonas Savimbi said in this connection: 'We have whites who are not Portuguese. They are technicians who came to help us. Their nationality is of no importance.'

In any case the presence of South African elements on the side of UNITA just as the presence of certain others can no longer be doubted. A young Angolan told us that he served as interpreter for fifteen Americans charged with training young recruits... at the Capolo military base, some 60 kilometres from Silva Porto. This information has been confirmed by Zaire soldiers fighting on UNITA's side.

And here is testimony by someone well acquainted with the situation in Angola. He is John Marcum, the American who was adviser to Tshombe and Roberto. In the *Foreign Affairs* article from which I had already quoted, he wrote: "In late October, ... in response to the desperate straits of an unarmed UNITA, South Africa intervened.... It is undoubtedly true that UNITA had welcomed the South African intervention. Moreover, it appears that Zaire and Zambia, both economically dependent on South Africa, secretly encouraged South African intervention, although neither could afford politically to acknowledge this...."

It came to pass that I arrived in Angola just a few days after Ryszard Kapuściński, correspondent of the Polish News Agency, returned to Luanda from the south of the country where he witnessed the massive invasion of South African troops into Angola in the vicinity of Pereira d'Eça. He told me that a South African motorised column passed through Pereira d'Eça and that the MPLA garrison numbering approximately 50 men was unable to put up an organised resistance against the enemy's overwhelming superiority in equipment and manpower. "A group of comrades from the

MPLA and I miraculously managed to avoid an encounter with the South Africans. I don't know exactly how many aggressors are taking part in the operation but I'm sure that there are not less than a thousand of them."

At the time he simply could not know all the details about the invasion of Angola by South African racialists. With time, however, fragments of information found their way into the West European and American press. And now, after piecing them together it is possible to get a full picture of the scale of the invasion.

According to an MPLA communique, the Cunene province was seized by South African units numbering 800 men. After that a column numbering 2,000 troops which was raised in South Africa and consisted primarily of mercenaries equipped with South African Panhard armoured cars crossed into Angola. Then, in October a group of South African regular troops consisting of a mechanised column with approximately 1,500 men entered Angola via Namibia.

On November 15 another South African Army unit numbering 1,500 men equipped with 100 US M-41 Walker Bulldog and French AMX-13 tanks crossed the Angolan border with the assignment to support in combat the column of mercenaries which had entered Angola in October. Air support was provided by a wing of Allouette 111 helicopters. Usually they were used to carry supplies, but during the operations in Angola they were outfitted with machine guns and took part in attacking MPLA detachments, while supplies were dropped to the columns by Namibia-based South African C-130 aircraft. Later the planes used the airports at Sá da Bandeira and Silva Porto.

In December still another South African unit comprising an artillery battalion and a tank battalion was moved into Angola.

How were the South African interventionists armed? In October and November the invading units had 36 Panhard armoured cars equipped with 90-mm guns, about 40 Marmion-Harrington light armoured cars, armoured personnel carriers and Unimog lorries, jeeps with 160-mm and 57-mm automatic guns and also approximately 25 M-41 Walker Bulldog tanks with 105-mm howitzers. The unit which crossed into Angola in December had 30 light armoured cars, 100 light tanks, mainly US M-41 Walker Bulldogs and French AMX-13, more than 100 armoured personnel carriers, jeeps with automatic guns and about 25 105-mm howitzers on Walker Bulldog tanks.

These units were to capture Luanda by November 11, the day when the country was to proclaim independence. But the MPLA troops stopped the enemy in the vicinity of Nova Redondo and prevented him from breaking through to the north. Thereupon South Africa moved another mechanised regiment numbering 3,000 men to Angola and also ordered fighter-bombers into action to offer tactical support for the land units. The London weekly *The Observer* noted that South African planes operated from the same base in the southern part of Zaire which was used by US transport and reconnaissance aircraft.

On December 9 UN Commissioner for Namibia, Nobel Prize winner Sean McBride, said in Paris that he was sure that South Africa used Namibia as a base for attacks on Angola. Initially South African troops penetrated 50 kilometres into Angola allegedly "to protect the dam" on the Cunene, then they advanced 100 kilometres and after that with the help of armoured columns penetrated 400 kilometres into the country.

All told there were at least 6,000 regular South African troops in Angola in December 1975. At the same time the authorities in Pretoria blustered that there was not a single soldier of their regular army in Angola.

Early in September, when the Angolan province of Cunene had already been captured and occupied by 800 South African troops, the South African Consulate which still functioned in Luanda categorically denied any armed interference by Pretoria. In the latter half of November, when there were about 4,000 regular South African troops in Angola, UNITA and the Pretorian authorities likewise vehemently denied South Africa's intervention in Angola.

On November 21, Reuter's correspondent Fred Bridgeland reported from Lusaka that Pretoria and the National Union for the Total Independence of Angola (UNITA) denied the presence of the South Africans, and went on to say that according to the South African Foreign Minister Muller his country had designated troops and equipment for Angola in order to protect the workers and the material values of the Cunene hydropower scheme on the border with South West Africa which was under the control of South Africa. Bridgeland added that debates on the policy towards Angola were going on in Pretorian higher circles and that officials favouring South Africa's military involvement were gaining the upper hand. Similar reports about the situation in the south of Angola were filed by other correspondents.

On November 23, 1975 *The Sunday Telegraph* wrote: "At least 100 South African 'advisers' are operating in Angola with the FNLA/UNITA forces, according to military strategists in Pretoria. They are there, it is said, because South Africa was 'asked to help'.

"The question of further South African involvement is still under consideration, although for the moment the policy of the Vorster Government is to wait and see which way the conflict goes.

"South Africa is reluctant to put in troops without the support of other Western Powers.... ...but the Vorster Government has not ruled out the possibility of major involvement, particularly if the FNLA/UNITA forces appear to be flagging and there seems a chance of tilting the balance in their favour....

"If South Africa did have to go into Angola in a major way, it is said, then it would involve 'a hell of a big operation' which would have to be mounted from the Republic itself. That is taken to mean a task force of several thousands...."

Several days later, on November 26, the US *Washington Post* analysing the situation in Angola in an article dispatched from Lusaka, reported that South Africa approached the United States and other Western Powers for more direct assistance to the forces in Angola which had the support of the west, and to increase the deliveries of modern weapons to the country. The paper wrote that as far as it was known the European countries which together with the US sent weapons to Angola included France, Belgium and West Germany, and added that the general opinion was that South Africa played the main role in terms of material and logistics support for combat operations.

On November 28 a UPI correspondent reported from Johannesburg that authoritative government circles in Pretoria acknowledged that the Republic of South Africa had joined the NATO member-countries in providing material and technical support for the armies of the anti-communist FNLA/UNITA groups in the form of military consultations. According to these circles, the correspondent went on, the

Republic of South Africa would help all those who asked it for help and that it would give advice to whoever asked for it. These circles also said that in Angola they were in the good company of the world's major powers.

What cannot fail to strike the eye is that all these reports either deny the presence of South African troops in Angola, or contain profound discourses on "possible" South African involvement in the "Angolan conflict". And if any admission at all is made about the presence of South African servicemen in Angola they are called "advisers" or "technical experts" of whom there were not more than 100. The reader has evidently taken note of the dates when these reports were sent. The last one, dispatched from Johannesburg, was dated November 28.

There is a saying that murder will out, and gradually more and more information about South African aggression in Angola hit the pages of the western press. Very often two newspapers, both of them British, for example, would print different reports: one would deny the presence of South African regulars in Angola, while the other would give a detailed account of the operations of South African troops in Angola.

A Reuter's report from Lusaka dated November 21 mentioned South African regular troops fighting in Angola hundred miles from the border and then stated that debates on the policy towards Angola were in progress in high official circles in South Africa and that officials favouring Pretoria's military involvement were reported to gain the upper hand. It also said that diplomats were unable to say exactly how many South African troops were in Angola and how much military equipment had been sent there. But, the report continued, these diplomats noted that many drivers of armoured cars in the columns heading towards Luanda were the South African servicemen and that the bulk of the armoured cars, or perhaps all of them, were South African. Reuter also said that the armed forces were moving from permanent South African military bases on the border of Southwest Africa and Angola, that the South Africans had set up an operational base in Sá da Bandeira in the south of Angola and begun setting up an advance base 550 kilometres from Luanda. . . .

These reports were filed when a 1,500-strong mechanised column was already operating in Angola after crossing the border on October 23, and when a second column also of 1,500 men was already in action in the south of the country. Bourgeois newspapers expressed the view that if some time in the future South Africa would become involved in Angola on a large scale she would form a task force of several thousand men. But these thousands were already in Angola at the time.

Afterwards some western ruling circles made every effort to dissociate themselves from South Africa's aggression, insisting that Pretoria acted on its own accord. In this connection an interesting admission was made by John Marcum in the above-mentioned article. "Although Mr. Kissinger has asserted it was 'untrue' that there had been any US 'collusion' with South Africa," he wrote, " 'high officials' in Pretoria have announced that South Africa's entry into Angola was made on the basis of an 'understanding' with American officials that the United States would rush sufficient supplies to counterbalance the weapons superiority of the MPLA ... and have expressed particular disappointment at Secretary Kissinger's inability to make good on his promises." And then he drew the following conclusion: "At the very least the United States connived at the South African intervention and sought to cooperate with it." Unlike Marcum, however, an unbiased observer would not have said that the United States "connived at" and "sought to cooperate with " South African intervention, because that would be putting it far too mildly. The USA and the Republic of South Africa had specific mutual commitments and they fulfilled them (an account of US participation in the aggression in Angola is given in the next chapter). The operation fell through because the MPLA with the support of the socialist countries, the USSR and Cuba in the first place, which faithfully fulfilled their internationalist duty, drove the aggressors out of Angola. But this happened later. At the moment, however, I should like to give an account of the events which took place following the entry of several thousand South African troops into the People's Republic of Angola. What were the relations between the South Africans and the FNLA and UNITA bands which they had taken under their wing?

On December 6, Savimbi's emissary in London declared: "We do not deny that we have South African instructors who help us with advice." If we were to believe him the five thousand armed to the teeth South African troops who captured whole provinces in Angola for the UNITA and the FNLA, were simply "instructors helping with advice".

On December 9, a few days after another column of South African troops numbering 3,000 men entered Angola, UNITA leader Jonas Savimbi organised a press conference in Lusaka. He defended the racialists and declared that the Africans were too emotional over South Africa's moves. He was compelled to admit the presence of South African troops in Angola, but promptly defended Pretoria by saying that South Africa had the right to bring her troops into the country.

Several days earlier a France Press correspondent reported from Pretoria that according to circles close to the South African Defence Ministry, technical assistance was furnished at the request of the UNITA and FNLA. It also quoted a senior officer as saying that South Africa had no reason not to help her friends who needed this help and asked for it.

On the day this report was dispatched from Pretoria two FNLA officials declared in Rome that South Africa's participation in the war in Angola became possible thanks to the UNITA which was an ally of the FNLA. And on December 5 an Associated Press correspondent reported that South African troops maintained daily contact with FNLA elements.

It was only on December 17 that South African authorities confessed their involvement in Angola. They had to make this admission because the MPLA announced that it had captured four South African soldiers between Sela and Quibala, 750 kilometres north of the Namibian border.

This news was promptly published in many countries. On December 18, 1975 *The New York Times* wrote: "South Africa announced today [December 17—*Ed.*] that four of its soldiers had been captured in Angola. . . .

"The announcement, issued by Defence Minister Pieter W. Botha in Pretoria, appeared to represent the strongest official admission to date of involvement in the Angolan conflict. . . .

"Authoritative sources had said previously that South Africa was providing military advisers and weapons to the two movements, which are based at Huambo and are also aided by the United States.

"The Defence Minister also announced that some army reservists would be called up early next year for three months instead of three weeks and sent to the so-called 'operational area' in the area of South-West Africa's border with Angola. He also said that enlisted men completing 12-month conscription periods would have to serve an extra month."

The interventionists were driven into a corner. At a press conference at the Information Ministry in Luanda the MPLA showed the journalists the four South African soldiers who had been captured east of Novo Redondo. They were Corporal Hannes Gernardus Terblanche and privates Robert Wilson, Graham Danney and Robert Wiehahn. Replying to journalists' questions they admitted that they were regulars of the South African Army.

Their detachment consisted of approximately 200 men and entered Angola from South Africa after passing through Namibia to conduct military operations against the MPLA. The prisoners of war admitted that they were getting higher pay while on their "mission" in Angola.

Higher pay for supporting the splitter FNLA and UNITA bands, higher pay for the savagely brutal treatment of the civilian population of Angola.

Much has been said and written about what went on in areas occupied by the interventionists. I also interviewed refugees who were fleeing to Luanda in October and November 1975, from the northern and southern parts of the country. Here are extracts from a diary which I kept in those days.

November 2, 1975

On November I met a group of refugees who arrived in Luanda from Sá da Bandeira. One of them was João Oliveira a worker from the small town of Mukanka just south of Sá da Bandeira. Here is a verbatim of his narrative:

"I know very little about politics. I'm over fifty and never attended all those meetings and rallies. And when neighbours began to say that it was dangerous to remain in Mukanka I didn't take them seriously and thought that I had nothing to fear. All of them supported the MPLA but I never supported anyone so what had I to be afraid of? Then I went to the market in Sá da Bandeira and stopped with a relative who lived on the outskirts. There were posters with a portrait of Agostinho Neto and the MPLA flag on the walls of all the huts there, and on my relative's hut, too. At about six or seven in the morning of the third day of my stay we heard shots fired. And soon afterwards many military lorries with strange-looking vehicles in front appeared on the road. My nephew said they were tanks. They were covered completely with green iron plates, the body, too, and many white soldiers with submachine guns were sitting on them. They shouted in a foreign language and kept on firing without a stop. We dropped to the ground to avoid being killed. When the machines passed, moving towards the centre of the town, I told my nephew that the worst was over. But before he had time to answer another column appeared. It was led by a small open car carrying the commanders, because one of them held a Portuguese banner. Now I know that they were mercenaries from the Portuguese Liberation Army. But then I didn't know what to think because the Portuguese soldiers had pulled out of our town and Sá da Bandeira a long time ago. Those in the second column also kept firing at the sides of the road. And when the last lorry approached, it suddenly stopped and several men jumped out and began to set fire to the roots of the huts. They also set our hut on fire, but we ran out and one of those who had set it on fire saw us and began to shoot. My nephew was killed outright. I fell and didn't move. Afterwards I crawled into the bushes and hid there for a day or even longer. Everything around was blazing.

"The following night I set out towards the north. On the way I met five other refugees who were also heading north. They told me what had taken place in the town the previous day, particularly on the outskirts. South African units and Portuguese mercenaries left the town and made in the direction of Benguela, and the town was taken over by UNITA detachments. The UNITA chiefs permitted their soldiers to do as they pleased for a whole day. They broke into houses, particularly those in the centre of the town where wealthy white people, Portuguese, used to live. They stole the few things that remained in the houses. They tied clothes into bundles, set fire to the furniture which they piled up in the streets. There was nothing to plunder in the huts of the poor people, so the UNITA men raped the women and killed the men. They also killed children. But they did not simply kill them. They tortured the people and only then put them to death. They shouted: 'There's a poster with Neto's photograph and MPLA flag on your hut. So now we'll hang you and then lay our hands on Neto'. And they hanged many. But they stuck knives and bayonets into even more people.

"I was lucky to get a seat in a lorry and now I'm in Luanda alive. I've lost everything and have nothing. I don't know how I'll live."

Such is the *modus operandi* of the interventionists and their puppets in Angola. It is no longer a secret that the bands of Roberto and Savimbi play a secondary role in the aggression. Incidentally, just a few days ago we, in Luanda, heard a Salisbury broadcast concerning Savimbi's recent meeting with Vorster in the capital of Namibia, Windhoek. The former agent of Salazar's secret police has placed himself wholly at the service of the South African racialists. So what doubt can there be about the true aims of Savimbi and his UNITA.

At present a fresh unit of interventionists activated in South Africa is on its way to Angola through Namibia. On top of that many Spanish and Portuguese fascists, PIDE agents, ex-servicemen of the US army who had fought in Vietnam, Belgian mercenaries, those who had fought on the side of the separatists in the Congo and Nigeria are arriving in Angola. This fascist rabble helps regular South African units and together with the UNITA and the FNLA floods Angola like a turbid torrent, causing death and destruction and bringing bondage to the people of that long-suffering land.

As the MPLA offensive developed the western press had to admit the fact of the joint FNLA/UNITA-South African actions more and more often. On January 22 *The New York Times* published an article from its correspondent Henry Kamm dispatched the previous day from the headquarters of the splitters in Huambo: "The real capital is nearby Silva Porto, the military headquarters of ... Jonas M. Savimbi. ...

"... The basic military decisions in the fighting against the Luanda forces, much of the field-level leadership, most of the heavy weapons and the logistical and communications structure are believed to be supplied by South Africa.

"South African troops are believed to be manning positions all along the front, which cuts across this huge country roughly along the 11th parallel, from the north of Novo

Redondo on the coast to about 10 miles south of Teixeira de Sousa on the border with Zaire. . . . Conversations here and in the port town of Benguela disclosed an organised South African presence all along the front.

"Residents in Benguela said South African convoys carrying armour, weapons and troops were driving through the town every night along the coastal highway. In the town itself, they said, South African officers occasionally come to dine with National Union commanders. . . .

". . . News photographers who have taken pictures of South African convoys passing through Huambo and others suspected of having done so had their films seized at gunpoint last week. . . ."

At about the same time UPI correspondent Raymond Wilkinson reported from Silva Porto that the FNLA and UNITA relied mainly on South African support and quoted a UNITA officer as saying that South Africans were very good soldiers. The officer added that they made a fine team. The South Africans had armoured cars and the UNITA infantry was advancing with them.

When facts about South Africa's intervention in Angola seeped into the press and it was no longer possible to conceal the aggression, the western propaganda media tried to convince the world public that South Africa was acting on her own, pursuing her own interests and that the FNLA and UNITA had no hand in it and therefore were the real representatives of the Angolan people.

Comrade Agostinho Neto spoke about these manipulations of the imperialist propaganda in an interview at the end of 1975. "At present, as we know," he said, "some imperialist circles in their propaganda are trying to draw a line between the South African racialists operating in Angola and the UNITA and the FNLA. By doing so they want to place the blame for aggressive actions only on the South African racialists and put the two separatist groups apart so that they would be able to form a so-called national unity government with the MPLA. In this way they want to misrepresent the actual state of affairs, although it is common knowledge that the South African troops invaded Angola precisely at their request."

And indeed, even the leaders of the splitter groups could not deny the presence of South African troops in Angola. UNITA leader Jonas Savimbi, for instance, admitted at a press conference on January 13, 1976 at the airport in Nairobi that South Africans were actually in Angola and were fighting on the side of the UNITA and the FNLA. But he tried to deny the fact that South African troops where in the country with the full approval of these two organisations.

The facts which subsequently came to surface proved that South African leaders did not act on the spur of the moment, but had devised far-reaching plans concerning the future of Angola. In December 1975, when thousands of South African troops were already deployed in Angola, Pretoria launched the construction of an airport in Upington in the north of Cape Province. Upington is near the Namibian border and the new airport was to have served as a base from which the South African Air Force would attack Angolan territory.

The South African military machine enlarged considerably in 1974 and 1975. In 1975 the republic's military expenditures reached US $ 1,300 million, a tenfold increase as compared with the 1965 figure. In addition to its 15,700 regular troops, 51,390 white recruits were called up in 1974 and by 1975 their number had reached 56,790. Moreover the country had 30,500 policemen and a so-called Citizen Force numbering many thousands.

The US *Washington Post* wrote on January 16, 1976: "... Pointer to South Africa's intentions is the continued call-up of members of the active reserve for extended military training and service in the 'operational zone'. The call-up is unprecedented in peacetime....

"South Africans who served in World War II and whose names were removed from the reserve list were notified this week that the removal had been an administrative error...."

In the beginning of 1976 a France Press correspondent in Johannesburg described how South African soldiers were dispatched to Angola. "Hundreds of South Africans mobilised for the Angolan war are continuing to leave the principal centres for training camps on the Angolan border.

"Several hundred soldiers from two Transvaal regiments entrained at the Johannesburg railway station on Thursday to the sound of bagpipes and applause of their weeping relatives and friends. The atmosphere reminded one of the departure of the troops at the outset of the Second World War.

"Some of the mobilised men received their calling up papers a few hours before departure and arrived at the station in civilian dress. Most of them were between 20 and 40 years of age and were married and had children.

"Their initial destination is Bloemfontain (in Orange Free State) where they will be put through intensive three-months' training prior to joining the forces already in action in the 'operational zone' [on the Angolan border or directly in Angola—*O. I*]."

The aggressors very quickly realised that the adventure in Angola was not a picnic as they imagined it would be. More and more relatives of the troops taking part in the intervention were informed of the death of their near ones. In January South African newspapers began publishing lists of killed servicemen and officers one of whom was a brigadier general. These lists were published until the end of February 1976.

Encountering the determined resistance of the patriots and sustaining a series of crushing defeats the South Africans began to search for ways of extricating themselves from the mess in which they had landed. On February 19 a France Press correspondent reported from Durban that "the United States had given South Africa 'certain assurances' before South African troops intervened in Angola". He quoted Senator Denis Worrall of the ruling Nationalist Party as saying that when South Africa decided to withdraw from Angola on December 24 "the Government was 'again requested by Dr. Savimbi and others to remain in. . . .' "

In April 1976 John Marcum wrote in *Foreign Affairs* that "Senegal and Ivory Coast (the latter extended landing rights to South African Airways in the midst of the Angolan crisis) reportedly joined Zaire in urging the South Africans not to pull out of Angola." That Jonas Savimbi requested South Africa to keep her troops in Angola was also confirmed by the South African press. The Johannesburg *Sunday Times* wrote on February 8 that Savimbi visited the "South African capital in December to appeal for more aid when Pretoria was 'wavering in its support' for his movement". The paper said that "information on Mr. Savimbi's trip had come from Senator John Tunney (Democrat, California) to the Sub-Committee on African Affairs of the US Senate Foreign Relations Committee following a fact-finding visit to Angola by two congressional aides Mark Moran and Bill Coughlin". It also noted that Savimbi flew to Lusaka where he conferred "with South African officials and military leaders on more aid in UNITA's fight against the MPLA".

At the close of 1975 it became clear that the patriots would rout the FNLA and UNITA bands and their allies, South African racialists and mercenaries from different countries, in the very near future. In the middle of December the FNLA detachments having sustained a shattering defeat at the hands of the national army of the People's Republic of Angola were rolling back farther and farther to the north of Luanda. The military situation in the south was also very favourable for the MPLA. In these circumstances the officials in Pretoria had to decide upon a definite course of action.

On December 11 a *Washington Post* correspondent reported from Zaire that an FNLA delegation would visit the United States and other NATO countries in an attempt to step up the shipment of military supplies and mercenaries from them.

In the middle of January, when a session of the Organisation of African Unity had failed to pass a concrete decision concerning Angola, the pro-government South African press said that the South Africa's involvement in Angola would continue. On January 15 *Die Transvaler* carried the banner headline "The Republic of South Africa Remains in Angola". The decision to increase South Africa's presence in Angola was taken on January 14 at a cabinet meeting chaired by Vorster.

At the same time official circles in Pretoria confidentially informed correspondents that the South African Government was inclined to enlarge military aid to the UNITA. In a dispatch from Johannesburg a France Press correspondent reported that in the first place South Africa would transfer additional helicopters to Angola and underlined that some of them were already being used in Angola by the combined UNITA/FNLA forces.

In the meanwhile the UNITA and FNLA in an effort to influence African and world public opinion tried to prove that South Africa intended to pull her troops out of Angola. On January 23 *The Guardian* wrote that according to Savimbi's henchman, UNITA Foreign Affairs Secretary Jorge Sangumba, South African troops and technicians began to leave Angola on orders from Pretoria and that the withdrawal would be completed by early next week. Several days later the paper asserted that the decision had been made three weeks earlier because the South African Government realised that in view of the low morale of the FNLA and UNITA Armed Forces which were considerably weaker than their opponents, the main burden of the war would fall on the shoulders of the South Africans.

But all this talk about South Africa's alleged decision to pull her troops out of Angola and that "they had already begun to leave the country" was pure bluff. On February 17, 1976 Member of the MPLA Political Bureau Lucio Lara declared: "Not a single soldier of the South African expeditionary corps which entered Angola in October last, has so far left our territory. Forced to retreat to the south they concentrated all their forces at the settlements of Rocadas and Pereira d'Eça where they have a powerful military machine and evidently intend to continue the intervention for an indefinite period. We cannot tolerate their presence and are not afraid to fight them. They want to perpetuate the war and they bear the responsibility for every fresh armed clash which may take place. Our objective is clear: to drive the invaders out of national territory to the last man."

This statement was indirectly confirmed by the South Africans themselves, when in an interview with *The Washington Post* South African Defence Minister Pieter Botha said that some 4,000 to 5,000 troops were patrolling "the whole area for which we are responsible. . . ."

There was another circumstance which could not be overlooked. On January 28 Defence Minister Botha tabled a draft bill in the South African parliament in keeping with which the South African Army would have the right to interfere militarily beyond South African and Namibian borders. According to a France Press correspondent in Capetown, parliamentary observers in South Africa regarded this move as belated manoeuvre designed to justify the military operations in Angola. Moreover, in the bill South Africa was called "Africa south of the equator", in spite of the fact that Kenya, Uganda, Tanzania, southern Somalia, Mozambique, Zaire, Gabon and Angola also lie south of the equator. And so with the adoption of this "law" South Africa appropriated the "right" to commit aggression against any of the above countries on a "legitimate basis".

Neither the romping of FNLA and UNITA canvassers across Europe and the United States, nor the propaganda campaign by South Africa and her followers, nor the adoption of new "laws", nor attempts by South Africa to hold on at least to the southern regions of Angola could prevent the logical outcome of the events. The aggressors and their puppets were beyond all help. And that was the inevitable conclusion at which the South African authorities arrived at long last. In March they were forced to withdraw from the last areas which they occupied in Angola.

This finale would have come much earlier were it not for the extensive support by NATO countries, the USA in the first place, for the South Africans and their hatchet men in the FNLA and UNITA.

The following chapter deals with US operations in Angola.

Chapter VII

The Dirty Tricks
of the Quiet Americans

The United States' supreme interests in Black Africa are in Angola.
(From a statement by Henry Kissinger in February 1970.)

"*Q.* Mr. Secretary.... There are no vital US interests at all in Angola. You said that publicly."
(Secretary Kissinger's News Conference of December 23, 1975. The Department of State Bulletin, January 19, 1976).

"*Q.* Would it be accurate to say that the US solicited South Africa's help to turn the tide against the Russians and Cubans in Angola last fall?

"*A.* I do not want to comment on that. The US Government can speak for itself. I am sure you will appreciate that I cannot violate the confidentiality of government-to-government communications. But if you are making the statement, I won't call you a liar.

"*Q.* Would it also be accurate to say you received a green light from

155

Kissinger for a military operation in Angola. . . ?

"*A.* If you say that of your own accord, I will not call you a liar."
(From Vorster's interview. *Newsweek*, May 17, 1976).

I shall not begin with an account of US activity in Angola and how US monopolies seized command positions in the Angolan economy. Neither shall I begin with 1961 when CIA agent Holden Roberto had his "pay" increased tenfold, to $10,000 per annum, for "collecting intelligence". I shall begin with an account of events which took place in the United States in January 1975.

On January 15, 1975 an agreement was signed in Alvor (Portugal) fixing November 11, 1975 as the day when Angola would proclaim independence. Likewise in January (that it happened in January is now common knowledge, but those who know the exact date prefer to keep silent, while those who do not know, stand to lose nothing) the Forty Committee, an important US Government organisation which studies intelligence information and in keeping with it draws up recommendations and plans for the future, met in Washington. The January session examined only one question—the situation in Angola. According to US political observers it was the first such discussion of the state of affairs in an African country since the mid-sixties. But in January 1975, no one in the US mentioned what the committee discussed at its meeting or that such a meeting had taken place at all.

What took place at the meeting came to light a year later on December 19, 1976 with the appearance of an article by Seymour M. Hersh in *The New York Times.* "The Ford Administration's initial authorisation for substantial Central Intelligence Agency financial operations inside Angola came in January 1975. . . . 40 Committee. . . agreed to permit the CIA to provide $300,000 clandestinely to Holden Roberto. . . . During the same 40 Committee meeting . . . the CIA unsuccessfully also sought authority to provide a $100,000 subsidy secretly to Jonas Savimbi, leader of the National Union for the Total Independence of Angola." Hersh quoted a "well-informed" Washington official's view concerning the Committee's decision to extend financial assistance to Roberto. The man said that he thought it very important and added: "That money gave him [Roberto–*O. I.*] a lot of muscle. He'd been sitting in Kinshasa for nearly 10 years and all of a sudden he's got a lot of bread–he's beginning to do things."

On January 7, 1976 *The Times* of London carried a report from its Washington correspondent Patrick Brogan: "Sources in Washington now say that the CIA first decided that steps must be taken to help the anti-Communists among the Angolan nationalists in January 1975. The Forty Committee which supervises the CIA, then approved sending $300,000 to the FNLA."

On January 6 *The Washington Post* carried a dispatch by Murrey Marder assessing the Forty Committee decision: "Senior US officials scoff at that," he wrote. "The $300,000 'was peanuts', a high CIA source said last week. But it was 30 times larger than any US annual sum ever given to Roberto. . . . President Ford is now reported to be blocking a report by the House Intelligence Committee which questions US motives in the $300,000 payment."

Several days later the paper returned to this theme. "Roberto has been the American favourite in Angola," it wrote. "His faction received $300,000 in political support through the Central Intelligence Agency in early 1975. American aid later was expanded to include support of the second anti-Communist faction, the National Union for the Total Liberation of Angola (UNITA)."

In April excerpts from a report concerning Angola which was drawn up by a Select Committee to Study Governmental Operations with Respect to Intelligence Activities, were published in Washington. It was disclosed that the Forty Committee met nine times between January 22 and December 11, 1975, to discuss Angola. The National Security Council met once, on June 27, 1975. In addition, an interagency working group on Angola met 24 times between August 13, 1975, and January 14, 1976.

I should like to draw your attention to the date–January 22–which in all probability was the day of the first meeting of the Forty Committee at which it decided to give $300,000 to Roberto. Here is how this fact was presented in the report of the Select Committee: "In January 1975 the administration decided to provide substantial covert political support to the FNLA faction in Angola." A delicately worded formula, indeed. What the Select Committee called "covert political support" was a $300,000 injection given to Roberto in order to make him torpedo the agreement signed in Alvor and begin the "physical extermination of the MPLA".

We know that Roberto worked in the sweat of his brow to deliver this money's worth, and organised a carnage in Luanda. But when the MPLA forces with the support of the capital's population drove his and UNITA's bands out of the city, the United States made yet another attempt to help him. In early June, 1975 the CIA prepared a proposal paper for military aid to pro-United States elements in Angola, the cost of which was set at $6,000,000. In July the Forty Committee and President Ford approved a revised programme costing $14,000,000. Coming into possession of a huge sum of money Roberto proclaimed the beginning of a total war against the MPLA.

August 8 was the day South Africa invaded Angola. Shortly before that Washington had decided to increase aid to the FNLA and the UNITA to $25,000,000. "In July, after Holden Roberto had announced his decision to seize power in Angola by armed force," wrote the Sierra Leone government paper *Nation* on August 23, 1975, "the United States announced that it was ready to increase its gratis aid by almost 100 per cent. Besides small arms, it said, it would deliver tanks, armoured carriers and lorries. They would be routed, with South Africa's consent, through Namibia and also through Cabinda under the guise of equipment for US-operated Gulf Oil."

Large consignments of US weapons were delivered from Kinshasa, capital of Zaire, to Carmona in northern Angola and the FNLA base at Negage by American Skymaster aircraft and Hercules transport planes. On August 15, the MPLA Information Chief Luis de Almeida declared that the FNLA "received large consignments of arms, including tanks".

There was another interesting circumstance. Approximately fifty per cent of the money allotted to the CIA went to pay for fire arms, mortars, ammunition, transport facilities, ships and communications equipment. But the figures cited in official reports compiled by various commissions and written down in the pay-sheets of the CIA, by no means reflected the actual cost of the weapons and ammunition sent from the USA to FNLA and UNITA bands. In February 1976 the American newspaper *Village Voice*, which was the first to publish the section of report dealing with Angola drawn up by the Select Committee, made the following observation: "The Committee has reason to question the accuracy of CIA's valuation of military equipment sent to Angola.

"A staff accountant on loan from the general accounting office has determined that CIA 'costing' procedures and the use of surplus equipment have resulted in a substantial understatement of the value of United States aid. Examples include 45 caliber automatic weapons 'valued' by CIA at five dollars each and 30 caliber semi-automatic carbines at 7.55 dollars. Based on a sampling of ordnance cost figures and a comparison with a Department of Defence procedures, staff advises that the CIA's ordnance figure should at least be doubled."

Used to having things in its own sweet way the Pentagon supplied the CIA with an unlimited amount of weapons and ammunition for them. The CIA valued each 45-calibre automatic weapon at five dollars, cheaper than the cost of an ordinary meal at a modest New York restaurant and entered this sum into its report on expended funds. Thus, for 12.5 million dollars it could have "purchased" 2.5 million automatic weapons, several hundred per each FNLA bandit. A simple trick, but by resorting to it the CIA could value each armoured carrier delivered to the UNITA and the FNLA at thirty or forty dollars and each helicopter at not more than a hundred.

Gradually the US became more and more involved in aggression against Angola. Weapons and ammunition were delivered directly from depots on US territory. For instance, this was how weapons were delivered to the FNLA on September 18, 1975. In the morning of that day several lorries drove into a US army depot in Anniston (Alabama) where they were loaded with crates containing mortar shells for US 4.2-inch mortars. The crates were brought to the nearest airfield and airlifted to Zaire on the same day. The plane's crew had documents prohibiting US customs, police and military officials from inspecting the cargo since the flight was conducted as a secret mission. Its code name "Project 612" became known later and stood for US military-aid programme to Zaire.

When MPLA units liberated the town of Caxito north of

Luanda from Roberto's bands, they seized a large quantity of these shells and the markings on their crates indicated that they had been flown from a US Army depot in Anniston on September 18. As regards "Project 612" information about it was published in the December issue of *Newsweek*.

That was how US military aid to the splitter FNLA and UNITA groups gathered momentum in the first eight months of 1975.

In November, when Angola had already proclaimed her independence, local and foreign journalists were invited to a press conference in Luanda at which they were shown the types of weapons and ammunition captured by the MPLA from the enemy and which had been brought to Angola from the USA and other NATO countries as well as the Republic of South Africa. The assortment included US bazookas with ammunition, anti-tank weapons, 130 and 106-mm artillery shells, 120-mm mortar shells, Belgian and British automatic fire arms, French anti-tank missiles and US grenade launchers of the type used by the US Army in the war against the Vietnamese people.

At the press conference MPLA officers showed the journalists the latest types of US weapons which had been delivered to Angola after November 1975.

Later it became clear that US arms deliveries constituted only one element of the extensive US military plans in Angola. Certain details of the Pentagon's plans were published by *The Observer* on January 11, 1976 in an article by David Martin who mentioned a "secret report" on South African and United States involvement in the Angolan war "prepared for a reputable international organisation".

According to the report "the American task force ... led by the aircraft carrier *Independence*, supported by a guided missile cruiser and three destroyer escorts ... was believed to have been placed under contingency orders between 15 and 23 November 'for a mission in the Angolan conflict'. The *Independence* carried 90 F-4 Phantom jets and was armed after November 15 with 'several hundred tons of napalm, Sidewinder missiles and anti-personnel fragmentation bombs in pods'.

"...In Portsmouth at the same time were two frigates, USS *Bowen* and USS *Ainsworth*, a guided missile destroyer, the USS *Farragut*, a submarine rescue ship, the USS *Kitty-*

wake, and two supply vessels *Kalamazoo* and *Denebola*."

"The *Independence*," the article said, "sailed on the night of 27-28 November and reliable sources say the *Bowen* and *Ainsworth* accompanied her.... According to the report, the task force stopped in the Azores to take on food, supplies and fuel in the first half of December. They were on 'full alert'."

The fact that the aircraft carrier and the other two warships were on full alert should be assessed in the light of the information leaked by the US Government, that US reconnaissance planes were making flights over Angola from the southern part of the Republic of Zaire to track the movement of the MPLA troops.

Bearing in mind the situation on the Angola front in the middle of November, it will become clear why the Pentagon decided to send a task force to Angolan shores precisely on November 15. The same article in *The Observer* noted that "initially officials in Washington, who knew about the impending attacks from Namibia [invasion of South African regular troops from Namibia into Angola–O. I.], believed the original columns would seep through to the capital, Luanda, defeating the MPLA.But in fact they were held north, overrunning the FNLA and taking its headquarters at Carmona".

While US naval ships loaded with hardware, napalm and almost a hundred jet planes cruised off the Angolan coast. President Ford commenting on the Senate's decision not to provide additional funds for deliveries of armaments to the splitter organisations in Angola dramatically exclaimed on December 19: "... How can the United States ... refuse any assistance to the majority of the local people, who ask only for military equipment to defend themselves? The issue in Angola is not, never has been, and never will be a question of the use of US forces. The sole issue is the provision of modest amounts of assistance."

What "majority" was the President talking about? The reply to this question was provided by Rene Lefort in the December issue of the French journal *Le Monde Diplomatique*. Noting that the US considered Angola just as the whole of southern Africa as its domain he wrote:"Today a small minority of Angolans and the majority of Zaireans, South Africans, former Portuguese colonists and servicemen in Angola and Mozambique are fighting the MPLA. MM. Holden

Roberto and Jonas Savimbi have practically lost all control over the military machinery. . . ."

Instead of foisting my personal opinion of US activity in Angola I should like to quote an assessment given by *The Washington Post* on December 24, 1975: "The United States, in its anti-Communist idiocy, seems hellbent on making another of the colossal blunders that brought us Vietnam.

"The reference, obviously, is to Angola. . . . Incidentally, the United States might have had a larger reservoir of Angolan goodwill to draw upon if we had given some small measure of support to the Angolans in their struggle to overthrow their Portuguese colonisers.

"Instead, we chose to maintain our alliance with Portugal. And now that the Portuguese are gone, we are throwing in with the South Africans."

The paper dotted all the "i's" and did not seek to create the impression that the United States believed that Roberto's and Savimbi's bands could have established control over the whole country. It directly said that by the end of 1975 the United States placed its stake on South African racialists. Yes, a sinister alliance was formed against the legitimate government of the People's Republic of Angola, which was recognised by dozens of countries on all continents on the first day of its independent existence. A sinister alliance in which the United States played a far from minor role. A sinister alliance which brought together the most diehard reactionary forces led by the South African racialists. In keeping with the joint plans worked out by the South African troops, Roberto's and Savimbi's bands and mercenaries, they intended to capture the capital, Luanda, prior to the proclamation of independence on November 11. And it should be said that at the end of October and the beginning of November the situation in the city was extremely unfavourable for the MPLA.

From My Angolan Diary
October 27, 1975

The situation in Angola is very complicated. This view is expressed by comrades from the MPLA and shared by the command of the group of Cuban military instructors. They arrived several days ago at the request of the MPLA leadership to help raise regular FAPLA units (Armed Forces of Liberation of Angola)—the MPLA Army. The Command of the Portuguese units still in Angola is apprised of this agreement.

So far only two correspondents from the socialist countries, Ryszard Kapuściński of the Polish News Agency and Igor Uvarov of TASS, were informed about the presence of the Cubans. Now I'm the third. Today they told me with a mysterious smile: "We'll take you along to meet our friends." We drove to a distant part of Luanda and entered a small two-storey house guarded by FAPLA soldiers and walked up to the second floor, where to my great surprise I heard voices speaking in the musical Cuban accents. Wearing their olive-coloured uniforms the Cubans were grouped around a map. The eldest of them was 35 years old.

Their mission was to help form several FAPLA battalions out of the volunteers who had just joined the army. The fact of the matter was that most of the commanders and soldiers who had many years' experience in guerrilla warfare against the colonialists, were in the north and in the central part of the country in detachments fighting against the FNLA and UNITA bands, while the newly-raised battalions were to be dispatched to the south to repulse the increasing aggression of the regular South African units.

The Cubans told us that they had been split up into several groups. One was training FAPLA fighters here, in Luanda, another in the vicinity of Salazar, the third was in Benguela and the fourth was in one of the garrisons in the centre of the country. The MPLA Army's main problem was shortage of weapons, particularly ammunition, and the second was the great length of the front of military operations. MPLA detachments were scattered throughout small towns and were out of contact with each other. The tiny MPLA garrisons which were in almost every town were naturally too weak to offer any serious resistance to the aggressors who were moving across Angola in several motorised columns each numbering more than a thousand officers and men.

FAPLA men, as the Cubans told us, were doing a great deal to put up defence lines in the vicinity of key centres. At Benguela, for example, five lines of defence had been built. But if the South Africans managed to reach, say, Benguela, and the roads in that part of Angola were quite good, then given the shortage of arms and ammunition the MPLA would have to perform a miracle in order to stop the enemy. "As regards the Northern Front," said the leader of the Cuban group, "the situation there as you know is very serious. The FAPLA is holding on to Kifangondo, while the enemy is within three or four kilometres away. He will attempt to seize Kifangondo or at least wreck the pumping station and then the situation in the town will become desperate. At present there are hundreds of thousands of people there and without water they won't be able to hold out for more than a week."

"The MPLA Command told us," said Ryszard, "that Roberto's bands and Zairean units are about to launch an offensive. But the Angolans are confident that they'll beat off the attack."

The Cuban smiled. "I'm sure they'll manage to do that. The fact is that the MPLA has several *katyushas* [Soviet rocket launchers–*Ed.*] and two of them are ready for action at Kifangondo. They have enough ammunition for only two salvoes, but I think even one will be more than enough for Roberto's bands."

I recalled how many years ago, during the Great Patriotic War, we, young Black Sea Fleet sailors who were in action with the ground forces drove back the nazis who had survived a salvo fired by *katyushas*.

"The MPLA," the Cuban continued, "must hold out for about half a month relying on its remaining ammunition. As soon as the MPLA proclaims independence in Luanda on November 11, our countries will come to the assistance of the Angolan people. At present the situation is complicated and there are certain issues of a diplomatic nature which have to be taken into consideration. Formally, the Portuguese are still in Angola and without the authorisation of the Portuguese Supreme Commissioner not a single plane with weapons will land in Luanda airport and not a single ship with weapons will enter the port of Luanda prior to November 11. The MPLA is well aware of this.

November 4

The day was packed with very interesting events, but it would be inexpedient if news about them appeared in the paper.

ri
ar
to
gı

eı
m
re
cc
A
si
ir

v(
N
te
P(
p(
pı
th
fe
m
w
th
le
eı
T:
is

ba
hu
of
ag
ga
tri
me
od
Ur
the
]
ass
cliε
em

Sı
A
aι
ui
ti(
aι
b(
cc
N
aι
o(
m
ki
m

Cuban seated i
cumstances it's
claimed, the c
have the legiti
and begin del
plans of these

November 6

Although we
nervous state y
on the night of
Kapuściński an
and I and Rys
we were to com
For example, w
tion in Luanda
dence. Ryszard
We decided tha
a bit strange s
radical change.
the forthcoming
to prepare our ı
ing.

To the surpri(
down in the lol
the telex which
gan perforating
job hammered t
continuing offeı
mercenaries and
Benguela and L(
erations conduct(
of the FNLA ba
appeared and toc

The day seem
formation Minis
tion about the S(
I also talked to s
a surprise visit i
up to Ryszard's
things including
at the desk becaı

In the morning the telephone in my hotel room rang. Our friends in the centre of Cuban instructors had news which they wanted us to know and invited us to come over. Fifteen minutes later Kapuściński, Uvarov and I were at the centre. Unfortunately the news was alarming. An hour ago there was a radiogram from Benguela which said that a column of South African regular troops had broken through three lines of defence at the approaches to the town. The situation was critical. The MPLA elements defending the town were running out of ammunition. If the South Africans pierce the last defence line and seize the town, the neighbouring port, Lobito, would also fall. And the distance between Lobito and Luanda was only 659 kilometres. It was flat country, ill-suited for defensive operations and the interventionists' armoured columns could reach the capital within three or four days.

Four days. That means that the South Africans and the mercenaries as well as UNITA and FNLA bands could break through to the capital either on the eighth or the ninth, two days prior to the date set for the proclamation of the country's independence. The MPLA had well-trained personnel capable of handling all types of weapon, but they could be put to little use because of the great shortage of weapons and ammunition. And no deliveries could be expected before the proclamation of independence.

We returned to Hotel Tivoli in low spirits.

At eight in the evening we listened to latest bulletin of news from the front. The announcer reported heavy fighting in some sectors of the Southern and Central fronts, but of course, there was no news about the situation in the area of Benguela. An hour later the telephone rang. Once again we were invited to the centre of Cuban instructors. Our first thought was that Benguela had fallen to the enemy.

As we drove to our destination it began to rain. What was a fine drizzle gradually developed into a regular tropical downpour. At the centre we learned that the leaders of the group of Cuban instructors were leaving for a meeting with Comrade Neto and that if we wished we had his permission to join them.

We arrived at his residence at about 11 o'clock. Neto received us without delay. In the ten days since my arrival in Luanda it was my first meeting with the MPLA chairman.

First a few words about the dimension of the recruitment campaign. Every once in a while in December 1975 and January and February 1976 the US, British, Belgian and French press reported the departure of yet another group of foreign mercenaries to Angola: "Thirty mercenaries have flown to Angola today", "It is expected that 96 mercenaries will go from London to Kinshasa to take part in operations on the side of the FNLA". At first glance such reports created the impression that these were limited operations and could have no effect on the situation in Angola. But this false impression disappeared as soon as the sums expended on "operation mercenaries" became known. In the beginning of February *The Sunday Telegraph* newspaper published in London said: "More than 10 million pounds ($20 million), mainly from the American Central Intelligence Agency (CIA), is to be spend on employment of British mercenaries in Angola." The CIA planned to spend $20 million in Britain alone. It should be borne in mind, however, that this operation was conducted in other European countries as well, and that its main centre was neither in Britain nor Belgium, but in the United States itself.

The CIA assigned the dirty work of directly recruiting the mercenaries not only to anti-communist organisations with which it had long-standing connections but also to a number of dummy "firms" which it established for this purpose. In Britain the main recruiting centre was a firm called Security Advisory Services (SAS) headed by certain declassed elements, including John Banks and Leslie Aspin. Judging by the fact that Banks had more than half a million dollars at his disposal to pay for men and materiél SAS was a pretty large enterprise.

In the United States the CIA set up some half a dozen dummy organisations for recruiting mercenaries. One of them called Co-op for Soldiers of Fortune was run by the American James Scott, who gave preference to veterans of the Vietnam war. In order to qualify the applicants had to know how to drive a tank, handle a large-calibre machine gun, or pilot a helicopter.

An organisation calling itself The Afro-American Technical Assistance to Angola operated in various states and its main recruiter of mercenaries was Larry Mitchell. Himself a Black and a veteran of the Vietnam war, Mitchell signed up only Blacks, primarily from among Cuban counter-revo-

And a similar notice in a British
newspaper

The victims of FNLA and UNITA
cutthroats

Mercenaries taken prisoner by
the MPLA

that they were clo:
naries.''

And when repor
than $20 million on
Angola against the
press, US Defence
US television. Accoı
refute these reports
these $20 million w
to go into details.
the CIA, powerful
operations without
of the US Armed :
African *Rand Dail*
techniques of the r
American and othe:
US units who have :
Army and voluntee
camps in Zaire and
procedure was follo
in their letters of ı
mercenaries in Angc
"volunteers" and w
other fact cited in tl
operation: ''...Recr
than 150 helicopter
ron of 13 helicopte
missiles. These airc
France to Angola.''

The US Armed Fo
the training of the :
itor wrote in Janua
Americans who had
tually all former se
dochina''. The pape
group underwent tı
Georgia, military a:
of the 197th Infant
School, and of the
there also for Range
ments of parachute j

"The vast trainin
source as having the

lutionaries who had emigrated to the United States. Mitchell
had his headquarters in the state of Maryland where he opened
a recruiting centre in Mount Rainier. A *Washington Star
News* correspondent visited the recruiting centre and interviewed Mitchell who told him that by the end of January he
had already enlisted about 200 men from the US capital.
According to Mitchell each mercenary was paid $1,500 a
month of which $500 were paid out as pocket money and
$1,000 were deposited on a special account in a Swiss bank.
When the correspondent asked him who financed the operation Mitchell shrugged his shoulders and said that only the
CIA could afford to spend such sums.

In California mercenaries were recruited by a company
calling itself El Kamas Enterprises in Anaheim, 120 kilometres north of San Diego. The head of the recruiting "firm"
said that the name El Kamas was taken from the code
name of a US organisation which operated in Indochina.

In the town of Highlands mercenaries were recruited by
Anubis Ltd.

The Hartford Times published in Hartford, Connecticut,
wrote about an organisation named Black Dragons which
recruited American ex-servicemen as mercenaries in the operations against the People's Republic of Angola. One of its
members said that 387 Vietnam war veterans, both black
and white, were ready to fly to Angola. According to the
paper he said that he intended to recruit 2,500 American
military veterans each of whom would get $1,200 a month,
but refused to divulge the source of the money to pay the
men and purchase the weapons.

The CIA established other dummy organisations such as
Unilever and Allied Chemical Personnel which recruited
mercenaries and sent them to Angola under the guise of
specialists and technicians.

In addition to dummy "firms" the CIA used existing organisations notorious for their anti-communist views. One
of them was the Congress of Racial Equality (CORE). "The
Congress of Racial Equality," wrote *The Washington Post*
on December 12, 1975, "has been recruiting black American
military veterans for service as mercenaries in the civil war
now raging in Angola.... CORE Chairman Roy Innis admits that his civil rights organisation is recruiting black
veterans for Angola.... CORE, which had headquarters in

New York, wa
struggle durin
has redirected
of 'black natic
"US intelli
the CORE re
a growing Ce
the military f
ation of Ang
dependence of
At the end
from the capi
the country a
Vietnam war
Southern Ang
The top me
their connecti
made no secr
hiring merce
Haigh wishin
of his Security
that he had
the United St
of Zaire, whil
ing with dolla
That the S
took its order
US Embassy
had been sma
Major James
and fulfilled
agent Lawren
London and w
These men gu
which recruite
Shortly bef
Angola, Calla
sentenced for
trial in Luand
Embassy in P
sistance to the
CIA agents w
in the US Emt

PROGRESS PUBLISHERS IS PREPARING
FOR PRINT

PAVLOVSKY V. *The Road to Stable Peace in Asia.*
Soviet Foreign Policy and International Relations Series.

The author, who is a diplomat writing on international affairs, tells about the important Soviet initiative for the establishment of a security system in Asia, an initiative stemming from the very nature of the Soviet Union's Leninist peaceful foreign policy. The author shows how the Peking leaders and other opponents of a constructive solution to this vital international problem have sought to frustrate the search for realistic ways to establish a security system, and also gives a good idea of the support the Soviet peace initiative has mustered across the continent.

74